ADOBE CREATIV

User Guide

Unlocking Your Creative Potential with

Adobe Creative Cloud

Ella Brown

Table of Contents

INTRODUCTION

Adobe software has traditionally been regarded as an industry standard for creative design and development. Adobe develops tools that make it simple to build astounding designs and projects. It gives users access to a collection of software used for graphic designs, video editing, web development, photography and cloud services it also includes products such as Photoshop illustrator, InDesign, Dreamweaver, lightroom and acrobat pro. Each software in Creative Cloud may be used alone, or you can combine them using Adobe Bridge, a separate program that lets you manage files with thumbnails, metadata, and other organizing features.

A single monthly subscription to Adobe Creative Cloud provides access to the whole array of Adobe products and more. Love print? Are you curious about websites and iPad apps? Are you prepared to edit video? You can do it all. In addition, Creative Cloud users get immediate access to newly announced goods and unique updates. And with cloud storage and the flexibility to synchronize to any device, your files are always accessible.

Creative Cloud is accessible to both individuals and teams. The first is Creative Services, which are hosted services you may use in your production process and content distribution.

The second aspect is Digital Publishing, which allows cloud-based publication of rich material to tablets. And the third category is Business Catalyst, which facilitates the building and operation of websites for small companies by providing prebuilt services for e-commerce, customer relationship management, and social media integration. Over time, more services will be introduced.

The second pillar is Creative Community, which is the global network of creative individuals (like you!) that helps you to connect with other creative people more easily - it's a place to share, communicate, and inspire each other with your work. The community is an integral component of our whole ecosystem, as well as the cloud. In the core of this is the Creative Cloud's web presence, which is located at creative.adobe.com.

And one of the nice things about it is that it supports all the file types you need in your creative work, including PSD, InDesign, and Illustrator files. Although other cloud services may display a symbol denoting the file type, this service displays the real content and allows context-sensitive interaction with it. It is a profound comprehension of creative stuff.

And finally, the third pillar is Creative Apps, which enable you to produce not only on personal PCs but also on mobile devices, all of which are linked through Creative Cloud. This includes Proto, Kuler, Debut, Collage, Carousel, Ideas, and Photoshop Touch, as well as a whole new suite of Adobe touch programs designed to work on tablets and other mobile devices. In addition, subscription gives access to all Adobe desktop creative programs, including Photoshop, Illustrator, Dreamweaver, Premiere, InDesign, and maybe Lightroom and more.

As part of your subscription, you may download and install any of these programs, and they are all linked to Creative Cloud through desktop sync. They also interface with touch applications, and data may be transferred between desktop and touch while working.

You may produce a variety of goods with the Adobe Creative Cloud tools, including artwork, page layouts, websites, photographic compositions, video, and 3D pictures.

Incorporating the CC programs expands the designer's potential outcomes. Don't worry about the complexity of the programs; simply come up with your ideas and start producing!

INTRODUCING ADOBE CREATIVE CLOUD

With the Adobe Creative Cloud release, you have access to the creative tools necessary for printed documents, online documents (including e-books), and interactive applications.

Adobe Creative Cloud's diverse software allows you to create anything from an interactive e-commerce website to a printed book. Each Adobe Creative Cloud application functions independently as a robust tool. When you combine all the applications, including Adobe Bridge, you have an unrivaled dynamic workflow.

This minibook demonstrates the many features shared by all Creative Cloud applications. There is uniformity in color, file formats, and text editing, as well as preferences for rulers and guides, across all CC applications.

This minibook also explains where to find the new features and how to utilize them to save time. In this book you are introduced to each component of Adobe Creative Cloud and learn what you can create with each of these potent tools.

Presenting InDesign CC

InDesign is a feature-rich and versatile page layout program. Using InDesign, you can create aesthetically pleasing page layouts. You may also exercise comprehensive control over your photographs and export them as Acrobat PDFs or other interactive documents. You may use InDesign to

- ❖ Use photos, text, and even rich media to create distinctive layouts and designs.

- ❖ Import native Photoshop and Illustrator files to create InDesign layouts that make use of transparency and blend modes.

- ❖ Export your work as a complete book, complete with chapters, sections, and automatically numbered pages.

- ❖ Produce interactive PDF files.

- ❖ Make drawings using the software's standard drawing tools.

InDesign is intended for layout professionals, but it is also simple enough for beginners to use. You can import text from word processing applications (such as Microsoft Word, Notepad, or Adobe InCopy) and tables (for example, from Microsoft Excel) into your papers and combine them with existing artwork and photos to create a layout. Importing, organizing, and exporting work are typical InDesign operations.

You have extensive control over your work throughout the whole process, whether you're working on a small one-page brochure or a complete book with more than 800 pages.

If you're already familiar with InDesign, you should read Book II, Chapter 1, to learn about some of the additional capabilities InDesign CC offers, such as the ability to produce e-pubs.

The use of Illustrator CC

Adobe Illustrator is the premier vector-based graphics program on the market.

Illustrator allows you to create layouts, logos for print,and vector-based pictures that can be loaded into other applications like Photoshop, InDesign, and Flash. Illustrator is geared for both graphics experts and online users. Adobe also allows you to produce files simply and quickly by storing Illustrator projects as templates (so that you may reuse designs effectively) and by using a specified library and document size.

Illustrator also connects with the other Adobe Creative Cloud products by allowing you to simply produce PDF documents inside Illustrator.

In addition, Illustrator files are compatible with Photoshop, InDesign, and Adobe's After Effects application for special effects. Illustrator helps you enhance your interactive documents by including Flash capabilities that provide you with the tools you need to create interactive Flash creations.

These are some examples of what you can create and accomplish using Illustrator:

- ❖ Produce technical drawings (for example, floor plans or architectural designs), logos, illustrations, posters, packaging, and online graphics.
- ❖ Apply effects to vector pictures, such as drop shadows and Gaussian blurring.

- ❖ Improve your artwork by making your own personalized brushes.
- ❖ Align text along a route so that it curves in an engaging manner.
- ❖ Format text into multicolumn brochures; content flows automatically from column to column.
- ❖ With graphing tools, create charts and graphs.
- ❖ Generate gradients that may be imported and altered in other applications, including InDesign.
- ❖ Make documents fast and effortlessly with Illustrator, utilizing existing templates and integrated stock visuals.
- ❖ Save a drawing in almost any graphic format, such as Adobe PDF, PSD, EPS, TIFF, GIF, JPG, and SVG.
- ❖ Save your Illustrator files for the web using the Save for Web dialogue box, which allows you to generate GIF, HTML, and JPG files.
- ❖ Save Illustrator documents as 128-

bit encrypted PDF files.

❖ Export assets as Flash symbols.

Introduction to Adobe Photoshop CC

Photoshop is the primary program for manipulating bitmap pictures for web designers, multimedia pros, and photographers.

You can manage and modify photographs using Photoshop by adjusting color, manually manipulating photos, and even merging many photos to create new effects. Instead, you may use Photoshop as a painting application to create pictures and graphics aesthetically.

Even more, Photoshop features a file viewer that allows you to effortlessly manage your photographs by assigning keywords and searching for them based on their information.

You may construct intricate text layouts in Photoshop by arranging text along a path or inside objects. You can edit the text after it has been placed along a path; you can even edit the text in other programs, such as Illustrator CC.

Join text and images into unique designs or page layouts.

Sharing images from Photoshop is easy to do. You can share multiple images in a PDF file, create an attractive photo gallery for the web with a few clicks of the mouse, or upload images to an online photo service. You can preview multiple filters (effects) at once without having to apply each filter separately.

Photoshop CC also supports various artistic brush styles, such as wet and dry brush effects and charcoal and pastel effects. Photoshop also has some great features for scanning. You can scan multiple images at a time, and Photoshop can straighten each photo and save it as an individual file.

It's hard to believe that Photoshop can be improved upon, but Adobe has done it again in Adobe Photoshop CC. Book IV shows you the diverse capabilities of Photoshop. From drawing and painting to image color correction, Photoshop has many uses for print and web design alike.

Working with Acrobat XI

Acrobat XI Pro is aimed at both business and creative professionals and provides an incredibly useful way of sharing, securing, and reviewing the documents you create in your Creative Cloud applications.

Portable Document Format (PDF) is the file format used by Adobe Acrobat.

It's used primarily as an independent method for sharing files. This format enables users who create files on either Macintosh or PC systems to share files with each other and with users of handheld devices or Unix computers.

PDF files generally start out as other documents, whether from a word processor or a

sophisticated page layout and design program.

Although PDF files can be read on many different computer systems using the free Adobe Reader, users with the Professional or Standard version of Adobe Acrobat can do much more with PDF files. With your version of Acrobat, you can create PDF documents, add security to them, use review and commenting tools, edit documents, and build PDF forms. Use Acrobat to perform any of the following tasks:

❖ Create interactive forms that can be filled out online.

- ❖ Allow users to embed comments within the PDF files to provide feedback. Commentary can then be compiled from multiple reviewers and viewed as a single summary.
- ❖ Create PDF files that can include MP3 audio, video, SWF, and even 3D files.
- ❖ Combine multiple files into a single PDF and include headers and footers as well as watermarks.
- ❖ Create secure documents with encryption.
- ❖ Combine multiple files into a searchable, sortable PDF package that maintains the individual security settings and digital signatures of each included PDF document.
- ❖ Use auto-recognize to automatically locate form fields in static PDF documents and convert them to interactive fields that can be filled electronically by

anyone using Adobe Reader software.

❖ Manage shared reviews—wwithout IT assistance—tto allow review participants to see one another's comments and track the status of the review. Shared reviews are possible through Acrobat Connect, formerly Breeze.

❖ Enable advanced features in Adobe Reader to enable anyone using free Adobe Reader software to participate in document reviews,

fill and save electronic forms offline, and digitally sign documents.

❖ Permanently remove metadata, hidden layers, and other concealed information and use redaction tools to permanently delete sensitive text, illustrations, or other content.

❖ Save your PDF document to Microsoft Word.This feature is a treasure! You can take advantage of improved functionality for saving Adobe PDF files as Microsoft Word documents, retaining the layout, fonts, formatting, and tables.

❖ Enjoy improved performance and support for AutoCAD. Using AutoCAD, you can now more rapidly convert AutoCAD drawing files into compact, accurate PDF documents without the need for the native desktop application.

Want to discover other great Acrobat improvements? Read Book V to find out all about Acrobat and PDF creation.

Introducing Dreamweaver CC

Dreamweaver CC is used to create professional websites quickly and efficiently, without the need to know or understand HTML (HyperText Markup Language). You can work with a visual authoring workspace (commonly known as "Design view"), or you can work in an environment where you manipulate code.

Dreamweaver enables you to set up entire websites of multiple pages on your hard drive, test them, and then upload them to a web server. With the Dreamweaver integration capabilities, you can create pages easily that contain imagery from Adobe Illustrator, Photoshop, and Flash.

Dreamweaver also has built-in support for CSS (Cascading Style Sheets), a language that allows you to format your web pages and control text attributes such as color, size, and style of text. CSS gives you control over the layout of the elements on your web pages.

Go to Book VI to find out how to use Dreamweaver CC to create exciting websites that include text, images, and multimedia. Read Book VI, Chapter 1, to learn about some of the important tools you will use in Dreamweaver, including an easy-to-use interface, tools to help you write CSS, and features to help you develop for mobile and HTML5.

Moving into Adobe Flash Professional CC

Flash's stunning motion graphics, visual effects, and interactivity have made it the industry standard for creating Web sites, game presentations, and interactive learning tools.

Create graphics and type in Flash with its comprehensive set of drawing tools, and then put them in motion with timeline-based animation, movie clips, and interactive buttons. Add photos, sound, and video for an even richer experience, or use Flash's built-in scripting language, ActionScript, to create complex interactive environments that stand out.

The most recent versions of Flash have continued to revolutionize the way websites, presentations, and rich Internet applications are built. Flash offers intuitive drawing tools, advanced video features, effects filters, and mobile export workflows for just about any creative endeavor. Turn to Book VII to discover how to use Flash to create drawings and animations, how to use ActionScript to create interactive web pages, and more.

Welcome to Fireworks CC

In the Creative Cloud applications, you have a tool for creating web graphics. Fireworks is a much-needed tool in the Creative Cloud package because it offers features that allow you to create assets necessary for web and application design.

You may wonder why Fireworks is included when the Creative Cloud already includes two other image-editing programs, Photoshop and Illustrator.

Among other things, Fireworks is useful for prototyping web page designs and creating on-screen assets for both web pages and applications using both bitmap and vector images.

Use fireworks to

- ❖ Evaluate file formats before exporting website visuals.

- ❖ Develop rollovers, animations, and pop-up windows.
- ❖ Generate picture slices using HTML tables or CSS.
- ❖ Create website wireframes and prototypes using the template and page features.

Learn more about the useful web-building tools in Fireworks in Book VIII.

Passage across the Adobe Bridge

Adobe Bridge is a truly remarkable application, especially within the Creative Cloud release, as the processing speed has been significantly enhanced and new features are available, including the ability to utilize the Mini Bridge, which is available in several of the Creative Cloud applications, including Photoshop and InDesign. Even though Adobe Bridge is part of Creative Cloud, it is not installed along with your other programs right away.

The first time you choose File Browse in Bridge from one of your other Creative Cloud programs, you will be brought to the Application Manager, where you may choose to install Bridge on your computer.

Mini Bridge works the same way as the full version of Adobe Bridge, but it stays open as a panel so you can quickly and easily access your files at any time.

Chapter 5 of this minibook provides further information regarding Adobe Bridge and Mini Bridge.

Combining Software

With so many excellent applications included in a single bundle, it's only natural that you'll want to combine them to create fascinating projects. You could design a book in InDesign (with images altered in Photoshop and illustrations generated in

Illustrator) and then develop a website using Dreamweaver for that material.

In a similar vein, you might want to turn a challenging PDF file into something that everyone can view online.

Instead, you may build a symbol or Flash text in Illustrator and finish the animation in Flash. All of the Adobe Creative Cloud tools are made to work together, which makes it much easier to do these things.

Integration of software is often helpful for all parties. Integration facilitates the streamlining of workflow between programs and, occasionally, team members. There are tools that allow native photos to be dropped into Dreamweaver, InDesign, Illustrator, and Flash. When choosing files for placement, Adobe Bridge allows you to browse them and examine detailed information about them, such as color mode and file size.

Obtaining Resources for This Book

Several of the files described in this book are accessible directly inside the Creative Cloud application sample folders. The route locations are established as they are referenced, making them straightforward to locate and utilize in the step-by-step examples presented. In addition to these example files, www.agitraining.com/dummies provides you with other files to explore and study.

Using common menus and commands

Many Adobe Creative Cloud menus, instructions, and choices are the same across all programs. To use Creative Cloud apps, you need to know how to navigate around these standard menus and dialog boxes.

You will note throughout this book that particular keyboard shortcuts are universal across programs. Its uniformity facilitates learning how to use the features and settings. This chapter presents an overview of the menus, dialog boxes, choices, actions, and preferences found in the majority of or all Adobe Creative Cloud products.

Identifying Common Menus

While working with Adobe Creative Cloud programs, you will notice that many of the choices on the main menu bar are identical. Even if you are unfamiliar with the program, key elements are easy to locate due to similar functionality.

Menu items include controls for the majority of an application's functionality. A menu item may also have characteristics linked to a certain job. You might, for instance, save from the File menu or modify your text from the Type menu. The following are examples of menu options that often occur in Creative Cloud applications:

❖ **File**: This section includes various functions that manage the document as a whole, such as generating, opening, saving, printing, and setting the document's general attributes.
Moreover, the File menu may provide options for importing or exporting data into or from the active document.

❖ **Edit:** This menu contains options and actions for modifying the active document. The commands include copying, pasting, and choosing, as well as choices for accessing preferences and configuring dialog boxes used to manipulate document sections. In addition to commands for spell-checking and object transformation, the Edit menu often contains commands for these functions.

❖ **Type:** This section includes choices pertaining to type and typesetting, including font selection, size, leading, and more.

❖ **View:** Provides choices for adjusting the document's magnification level. The View menu may also have choices for displaying the workspace in various ways, displaying rules, grids, or guidelines, and activating alignment snapping. Snapping facilitates the exact positioning of selection edges, marquee cropping, slices, forms, and pathways.

❖ **Window:** Includes choices mostly used to open and shut the application's accessible panels. You may also pick how to see the workspace and store a preferred configuration.

❖ Help provides the option to access the application's bundled help documentation. This menu may also include information on software updates, registration, and tutorials.

Each program contains extra application-specific menus based on the software's requirements. With the Photoshop Image menu, you can, among other things, resize the picture or document, rotate the canvas, and duplicate the image. InDesign contains a Layout menu that you may use to traverse the document, modify page numbering, and get access to tools for generating and updating the document's table of contents; these menus are discussed throughout this book as applicable.

Using Dialog Boxes

A dialog box is a window that opens when certain menu items are chosen. It provides more choices in the form of drop-down lists, panes, text fields, option buttons, check boxes, and buttons that allow you to modify settings and input the required information or data. You manipulate the program or your document in a variety of ways using dialog boxes. When opening a new file, for instance, you generally utilize the Open dialog box to pick a file to open.

When you save a file, you use the Save As dialog box to set the file's location, name, and the command to save the file. Some dialog boxes have tabs as well. These dialog windows may have several parameters from various categories that are arranged into multiple tabbed sections. Typically, a dialog box has two buttons: one that performs the specified command and another that cancels and dismisses the box without taking any action.

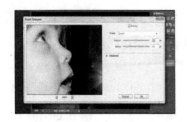

A Windows dialog box provides the same functionality as a Mac dialog box. For entering and selecting information in dialog windows, the same components and functions are present. Here are a few examples of tasks performed with dialog boxes:

❖ Save a file's updated version.

❖ Indicate your printing or page-layout preferences.

❖ Configure the preferences for the program you are using.

❖ Verify the spelling of a document's text.

❖ Open a new document.

REMEMBER

You are unable to use the program until the dialog box is closed. When a dialog box is active in an application, a pop-up window appears on the screen. Before you may continue using the program, you must close the dialog box. You may close it by making your selections and clicking a button (such as Save or OK) or by clicking Cancel to dismiss it without making any changes.

Experiencing Alerts

Alerts, which are widespread on every operating system and in the majority of programs, are similar to dialog boxes in that they are tiny information-containing windows. Nevertheless, warnings differ from dialog boxes in that their contents cannot be edited. Alerts are intended to inform you of something and provide you with one or more alternatives that you may choose by pressing a button.

For instance, an alert may warn that a certain choice cannot be made. Clicking the OK button often acknowledges and closes the notice. There may be additional buttons on the alert, such as a cancel button or a button that opens a dialog box.

 An alert can be used to confirm an action before it is performed. Sometimes, a warning or alert window will have a way (usually a checkbox) to tell it not to show up again. If you do something that always shows the warning, but you don't

27

need to see it every time, you might want to choose this option.

Understanding Popular Menu Choices

In general, each of the Creative Cloud apps has a variety of menu choices. Nevertheless, inside each of these choices are numerous other possibilities. Some of them open dialog windows, which are normally denoted by an ellipsis after the menu item.

The following menu items are available in several Creative Cloud apps and do similar (or the same) things or open similar dialog boxes:

❖ Creates a new document in the native file format. With InDesign, for instance, a new INDD file (the extension for InDesign documents) is produced by

selecting
FileNewDocument.
Sometimes, you
may choose the
type of new file to
create.

❖ Open: Opens a
dialog box in which
you may choose a
file to open from
your hard drive or a
disc.

❖ This command
closes the active
document. If it
contains unsaved
modifications, you
must first save
them.

❖ Save: Saves the
modifications to
the current
document.

❖ Save As: Saves a
duplicate of the
current document
with a new name.

❖ Imports a file into
the current
document, such as
an image or audio
file.

❖ Export: Exports the
current data to the
file format selected.
You may have to
choose between
several file formats
to save the current
data in.

❖ Copy: Copies the
selected data to the
computer's
Clipboard.

❖ Paste: Inserts the
clipboard's

contents into the current document.

- ❖ Undo: Undoes your most recent action inside the program. For instance, if you just construct a rectangle, it gets deleted from the page.
- ❖ Redo: Repeats the actions performed by the Undo command. For instance, if you deleted the rectangle you drew, the Undo command would restore it to the page.
- ❖ Zoom In: Enlarges the document so that its contents

can be seen and edited more closely.

- ❖ Zoom Out: Resizes the display to display more of the document at once.
- ❖ Help: Opens the current application's Help documentation.

About Contextual Menus

The contextual menu is an exceptionally helpful and rapid method for making choices or issuing instructions, and it is accessible in a wide variety of programs. Context-sensitive menus may contain some of the most useful instructions you may find yourself selecting on a regular basis.

A contextual menu is similar to the menu types described in the preceding sections; however, it is context-sensitive and appears when you right-click (Windows) or control-click (Mac) on an application element. Contextual indications indicate that the menu options are determined by the object or item on which you right-click (Windows) or control-click (Mac OS).

For example, if you open a contextual menu while the cursor is over an image, the menu will include actions that have to do with the image. Nevertheless, when you right-click (on Windows) or control-click (on Mac) on the document's backdrop, you are often presented with choices that impact the whole document rather than a specific piece inside it. So, you may pick common instructions, particularly for the specified object. Figure 2-5 depicts the contextual menu that displays in Photoshop when you right-click (Windows) or control-click (Mac) on an item.

Depending on which tool you choose from the Tools panel, the contextual menus in a document may be different. Before you can access some menus, you may need to select the Selection tool. Make sure the object is chosen before right-clicking (Windows) or control-clicking (Mac OS) to launch a contextual menu.

If you have a two-button mouse connected to your Mac, you can right-click to get the contextual menu. If not, control-clicking will open a contextual menu.

Using Frequent Keyboard Shortcuts

Shortcuts are key combinations that allow you to perform operations like saving or opening files or copying and pasting items fast and effectively. Some of these shortcuts may be found on the menus covered in the preceding sections. If the menu item has a key combination displayed next to it, you may use that combination instead of the menu to access the command.

For instance, if you enter the File menu, the shortcut for Save is Ctrl+S (Windows) or +S (Mac OS) (Mac). Instead of selecting FileSave, you may use shortcut keys to save your file. It expedites the execution of a certain instruction.

Table 2-1	Common Keyboard Shortcuts	
Command	*Windows Shortcut*	*Mac Shortcut*
New	Ctrl+N	⌘+N
Open	Ctrl+O	⌘+O
Save	Ctrl+S	⌘+S
Undo	Ctrl+Z	⌘+Z
Redo	Shift+Ctrl+Z	Shift+⌘+Z
Copy	Ctrl+C	⌘+C
Paste	Ctrl+V	⌘+V
Print	Ctrl+P	⌘+P
Preferences (General)	Ctrl+K	⌘+K
Help	F1 or sometimes Ctrl+?	F1 or sometimes ⌘+?

There are several other keyboard shortcuts that are not displayed on menus in each of the Creative Cloud programs. You may locate these shortcuts throughout the application-specific documentation. Learning shortcuts takes time, but the time you save in the long run makes it worthwhile.

Modifying Your Choices

While dealing with new software, it's essential to configure your settings. Knowing what your preferences can accomplish for you provides a strong understanding of what the program does. Every Creative Cloud app has various choices, but the Preferences dialog box in each application functions identically.

With each program, you may access the Preferences dialog box by selecting Edit Preferences (Windows) or Application Name Preferences General (Mac). To move from one subject to the next, click an item in the list on the left side of the dialog box.

You may control a large variety of settings by putting values into text fields using drop-down lists, buttons, check boxes, and other like controls. Preferences may be fairly extensive.

You do not need to know what each choice does or modify any of them. The majority of preference dialog boxes are fairly explicit in detailing which

34

functions they regulate and are thus straightforward to use. Adobe also adds a Description field towards the bottom of the dialog box on occasion. When the mouse is hovered over a certain control, its description appears in the Description section.

The categories of preferences that can be changed are listed in a list box on the left side of the various Preferences dialog windows. After modifying the parameters for this subject, pick a new topic from the drop-down menu and modify the options for that topic.

In certain apps, the Preferences dialog box may not include all configurable parameters. To alter the color settings in Illustrator, for instance, choose EditColor Settings to enter the Color Settings dialog box. When the mouse cursor is hovered over a certain drop-down list or button, an explanation of that control shows at the bottom of this really handy dialog box.

Figure 2-8 shows that you can change the color settings for all Creative Cloud apps at once by opening Adobe

Bridge choosing EditColor Settings.

With a number of Creative Cloud products, you can choose the main settings for your document, such as the page size, the number of pages, and whether the page is in landscape or portrait mode. You can use the following command to get to these kinds of settings in each program:

❖ New   File: Dreamweaver
❖ Document   File Configuration: Illustrator   and InDesign
❖ Image⇨ Dimensions: Photoshop

Exploring Common Panels

The panel is a crucial component of working with the majority of Adobe Creative Cloud apps since it includes many of the controls and tools used while generating or modifying documents.

The core operation and function of panels in Adobe Creative Cloud products are relatively similar, and all panels serve the same purpose. Panels provide a great lot of freedom in organizing the workspace and the used components.

The job for which you use each piece of software and your degree of competence may influence which panels are now shown. This chapter provides an overview of how to operate with the Adobe Creative Cloud panels.

Comprehension of the Synchronized Workspace

The synced workspace is one of the first things you'll notice when launching Creative Cloud programs. All the programs have the same appearance and feature set to help you manage your workplace.

The tools of InDesign, Illustrator, and Photoshop are shown on a space-saving, single-column toolbar, and panels (explained in detail in the next section) are grouped in self-adjusting docks that you may broaden to full size or narrow to collapse the panels to icons.

Here are some navigation tips for the Creative Cloud apps' workspaces:

Figure 3-1: Click the arrows at the top of the Tools panel to show tools in two columns or one column.

❖ To extend tools into two columns, click the double right-pointing arrows at the top of the gray Tools panel bar.

❖ To collapse the Tools panel to a single column, click the two left-pointing arrows on the gray bar at the panel's top.

❖ Click the symbol in the docking area to expand a docked panel, as illustrated in Figure 3-2. The chosen panel grows but disappears when another panel is selected.

If you are having trouble locating the panel, you may choose it from the Window menu.

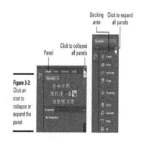

Figure 3-2: Click an icon to collapse or expand the panel.

* ❖ To expand all docked panels, click the double-arrow symbol facing left at the top of the docking area; to collapse the panels, click the double-arrow icon facing right in the gray bar above them.

* ❖ To undock a panel, just click the panel's tab and drag it out of the docking area. You can redock the panel by dragging it back into the docking area.

Panel Utilization in the Workspace

Panels are tiny windows inside a software that include controls, including sliders, menus, buttons, and text fields, that allow you to modify the settings or properties of a selection or an entire document. Moreover, panels may provide information about a section or the document itself. You may use this information or the panel's settings to adjust the chosen item or the document you're currently editing.

Whether you're using Windows or a Mac, the appearance and functionality of panels are comparable. Following are the fundamentals of dealing with panels:

❖ Open a panel: Using the Window menu, you may open a panel in Creative Cloud software. Choose Window, followed by the name of a panel.
For example, choose WindowSwatches to get to the Swatches panel, which is the same in many Creative Cloud products.

❖ Close a panel: To open or close a panel's tab or the entire panel, simply select the WindowPanel's Tab Name.A panel may include a close button (an X button in Windows or a red button on a Mac) that you can use to close the panel.

❖ Arrange the workspace: All Creative Cloud applications now provide workspace organizing options. Choose WindowWorkspace

Default to return to the default workspace, which restores panels to their previous positions. You may also open commonly used panels, reposition them, and save a customized workspace by selecting WindowWorkspace Save (or New) Workspace from the menu bar.

The workspace can now be opened by selecting WindowWorkspace Your Saved Workspace's Name from the menu.

Also, you can choose from a large number of presets that are made for different activities.

❖ Access the panel menu: As shown in Figure 3-3, you can access the panel menu by clicking the arrow in the upper-right corner of the panel. When you click the panel menu, you can choose from a number of options that are related to the tab you have chosen.When you pick an option from the panel's menu, it may perform an action or display a

41

dialogue box. Some panel menus only have a few options, but other panels may have a lot of related functions and, as a result, a long panel menu.

❖ Minimize/maximize: To minimize a chosen panel, just click the double-arrow "Collapse to Icons" button in the panel's title bar (if present). If the panel is undocked, you may double-click the tab inside the panel itself. This action either reduces the panel by half or completely. If it just minimizes partly, double-clicking the tab again reduces it completely. If the panel is minimized and the active tab is double-clicked, the panel will expand again.

You can work with panels that have different amounts of information, which simplifies the workspace and makes the most of the space on the screen.

Most panels have tabs, which allow you to arrange program information and controls into groups. Each tab in a panel has specific information about a part of the program. Many tabs can be found in a single panel.

The tab's name often indicates the sort of function it controls or information it shows, and it is situated at the top of the panel. Inactive tabs are rendered faint.

Moving panels

You may move panels anywhere within the workspace and add or delete individual tabs from a panel. Each panel clips to the next, making it simple to align panels side by side. Panels may also be overlapping. To snap panels together, drag the panel to a new place onscreen, as seen in Figure 3-4; the panel's top bar will become darkened to indicate that it is joining the group of another panel.

Move related tabs into a single, grouped panel to group them. Accessing various functions in your document becomes simpler since less time is spent looking for functions that are relevant to a certain activity. If you want to revert to the default workspace, choose Reset Workspace from the Window menu's Workspace section. By hitting Tab, you may conceal all panels. Press it again to reveal all the hidden panels.

Looking at common panels

Several panels are the same across Creative Cloud applications. While not every panel in every program has identical material, the vast majority have relatively comparable information. These panels are used in a similar manner, regardless of the software or operating system you are using.

Acrobat does not feature as many panels as other Creative Cloud applications. Instead, Acrobat depends on a system of menus and toolbars, including buttons and drop-down options. You may open dialog boxes in Acrobat that provide a variety of options for our papers.

The following panels are available in most, but not

all, of the Creative Cloud apps. This list outlines what each item may be used for:

❖ Color: Pick or combine colors for usage in the current document. There are a lot of color modes and ways to mix and choose colors in the Colors panel.

❖ Info: See information about the document or a specific selection you've made. The Info panel provides information on the size, placement, and rotation of selected items. You can't input data into the info panel. It shows information but does not accept it; therefore, you must utilize the Transform panel (explained in this list) to make any required alterations.

❖ Swatches: Make a collection of swatches that you can export and import into other documents or programs.You may keep frequently used colors and gradients in the Swatches panel.

❖ Tools: This key panel, commonly referred to as the

"toolbox" (and not present in all Creative Cloud apps), is used to pick tools, such as the pencil, brush, and pen, for creating objects in a project.

❖ Layers: show and select layers, modify layer order, and select objects on a certain layer.

❖ Align: Align selected items to each other or to the page itself. This lets you put things in a precise order.

❖ Stroke: Pick strokes and modify their properties, including color, width/weight, style, and cap. The software in use specifies which properties are modifiable.

❖ Transform: Show and modify the object's shear (skew), rotation, location, and size. You may modify each transformation's values.

❖ Character: Choose typefaces, font sizes, character spacing, and other type-related options for your works.

Using Common Extensions and Filters

Extensions, often known as plug-ins, are computer-installed or saved software components that function as add-ons to current applications. You may be able to utilize an extension to interface with another application, add functionality to a program (such as the ability to produce 3D text), alter the look of an item in your software, or add a 3D effect to a video clip. Filters may be used to modify portions of a document. Even if you've never used Photoshop, you're certainly acquainted with some of its most popular creative filters, such as Watercolor and Emboss. This chapter demonstrates how to utilize standard plug-ins, extensions, and filters with Creative Cloud.

Examining Frequent Extensions and Filters

Extensions are meant to add to what a program can already do and are often used for similar tasks in many different programs. Furthermore, extensions and filters may significantly accelerate the creative process. At the press of a button, you can add a stunning effect to your project that would have taken hours to create without the plugin.

On the Adobe website, you can find links to or extra filters and plug-ins for the products. Moreover, plug-ins are readily available for download on the web. These packages provide several results from a search. Adobe Marketplace & Exchange is a fantastic place to start: https://www.adobeexchange.com/. Afterwards, you may download and install an abundance of Creative Cloud application-specific tools.

The Photoshop filter is perhaps the most widespread sort of internet add-on. Some filters must be purchased before they may be downloaded and used, while others are free.

Installing extensions

You can install extensions in a few different ways. Sometimes you use an executable file: Double-click the file on your hard drive, and it automatically installs the software. This process is a lot like installing any other program on your computer, such as the programs in the Creative Cloud itself.

Sometimes individual files need to be placed in a folder first. In that case, you need to find the Plug-ins folder on your computer in the Install directory of the program the plug-in or filter works with. For example, if your plug-in works with InDesign on Windows, you have to find the directory C:\Program Files\Adobe\ InDesign CC\Plug-ins. You then copy and paste or move the files you downloaded into this directory on your hard drive. If your plug-in works with Photoshop on the Mac, find the folder on your hard drive: Applications\

Adobe Photoshop CC\Plug-Ins. Then copy and paste or move the files into the folder.

You can also take advantage of the Adobe Extension Manager CC application, installed automatically with the default Creative Cloud CC installation. Locate Extension Manager in your Programs (Windows) or Applications (Mac) folder and double-click to launch it. Select the application for which you want to install the extension, click the Install button to locate the extension you want to install, and click the Select button—you're on your way!

If you're unsure how to install a plug-in, locate instructions for the software that explain how to install the plug-in on your computer. You can find instructions on the manufacturer's website or bundled with the plug-in file in a text file (usually named readme.txt).

Plugging into InDesign

There are several plug-ins for InDesign that let you add to the features that are already there. These are some things you can accomplish with extra InDesign plug-ins:

❖ Correctly format sheets for a printer.

48

- ❖ Provide refined indexes and a table of contents.
- ❖ Generate powerful internal cross-references in your papers.
- ❖ Generate thumbnails and page previews for your documents.

Additional InDesign-created filters may facilitate the importation of particular items, such as text. When you import information into InDesign, text formatting is often lost.

While importing text, filters allow you to preserve the original formatting. These plug-ins

and filters are just a taste of what InDesign offers. Almost certainly, developers will produce many more software plug-ins.

Enhancing Photoshop

Many preloaded plug-ins and filters enhance the usefulness of Photoshop. You may discover extra filters and plug-ins to add new features to your papers, which will always offer intriguing effects. One plug-in, for instance, installs a variety of Photoshop filters.

- ❖ With Photoshop's filters and plug-ins,

you can enhance your images.

❖ Produce 3D text, objects, and effects with a variety of plug-ins.
Effects include drop shadows, bevels, and embossments that are more realistic than those in Photoshop.

❖ Use specialized masking techniques to create incredible choices of difficult objects like fur and hair.

❖ Use one of the tens of thousands of special effects (manufactured by a variety of firms) to enhance and edit photographs.

Add a frame from a library to your preferred pictures. This article only talks about a small number of the things you can do with Photoshop plug-ins, which often come with a variety of filters.

Several plug-ins have interfaces that can be changed. These interfaces usually have sliders, text boxes, buttons, and thumbnails that show how the filter is changing the picture.The design and number of functions of these interfaces are very different, but they are usually clear and easy to use.

Using Illustrator add-ons

There are several tools available to increase the capabilities of Illustrator. There are plug-ins that allow you to take 3D illustration beyond the capabilities of regular 3D features. Forms may be created from drawings, and 3D files can be converted to line drawings. Various plug-ins, ranging from basic to extremely complicated, enable you to do the following:

- ❖ Arrange the font families.
- ❖ Include popular icons, such as traffic signs, in papers.

Symbols are grouped in libraries that may be accessed directly from the Illustrator workspace.

- ❖ Import documents, including computer-aided design (CAD) files.
- ❖ Generate documents with interactivity.
- ❖ Work with patterns designed to create textures and backdrops.

After downloading and installing a few plug-ins, Illustrator's capabilities can be improved. When you just enter a value and click a button, simple projects become significantly more fascinating or difficult.

A custom brush is a good thing to download and put into Illustrator. When creating drawings and illustrations, you will then have access to a greater variety of brushes. You can install styles in Illustrator, which are often accessible for no cost. For Photoshop, you may even download and set up your own brushes.

Acrobat's capabilities are being expanded

Many Acrobat plug-ins facilitate project workflow speed and variety. You can use some of the available plug-ins to assist you.

- ❖ Update the documents' stamps.
- ❖ Include elements like page numbers and watermarks.
- ❖ Streamline productivity by providing batch processing solutions.
- ❖ Change file formats to expand the range of documents that Acrobat can create.
- ❖ Quickly and effectively with the Portable Document Format (PDF) in prepress.

The pages of a document can be batch processed (all at once) using one of the several Acrobat plug-ins that are available. While preparing PDF files, many Acrobat plug-ins can save you a ton of time. Plug-ins can spare you from having to complete a tiresome and repetitive chore because they are often made to be simple to use.

There are various third-party websites and the Adobe website where you can find Acrobat plug-ins.

Dreamweaver expansion

You can quickly and easily create web pages with Dreamweaver, but you can also expand the range of activities the application is capable of by adding additional tools. The process of building websites is also accelerated by these extensions (basically plug-ins). Dreamweaver plug-ins that are accessible to you

- ❖ Automatically add e-commerce modules to a website.
- ❖ Use Cascading Style Sheets and Dynamic HTML (DHTML) to produce aesthetically pleasing vertical

and horizontal menus (CSS).

- ❖ Add a pop-up calendar.
- ❖ Include PayPal on your website.

Using Filters and Plug-Ins

With Creative Cloud applications, you may add plug-ins and filters. For instance, a filter may enliven an already-existing photograph. After installing a plug-in that adds a variety of filters to Photoshop or Illustrator, examine the effects of each filter on your photographs.

Install some Photoshop filters (or Illustrator filters, or any other Creative Cloud product filter). When the installation has been completed and the computer has been restarted, if necessary, launch Photoshop and go to the Filter menu option. (Additional filters have been added to this menu.)

Follow these procedures to use a filter or plug-in after it has been installed:

1. **To test your new filter or plug-in, open a file in the relevant software:**

For instance, if you have downloaded a Photoshop plug-in that adds a new filter, open a picture that you want to apply an effect to in Photoshop. Choose a photograph with a large number of colors and/or contrast.

2. **Choose a filter from the Filter drop-down menu:**

Choose an installed filter from the Filter drop-down menu. You may also discover that a plug-in added a new menu item to the application; if so, utilize the new menu item to apply the effect.

3. **Make any necessary adjustments to the filter's (or plug-in's) parameters, then**

click OK to apply the effect:

Sometimes, a thumbnail preview is shown to demonstrate how a filter modifies a picture. With some filters and plug-ins, you may even use a custom interface to edit the document. Afterwards, you may adjust the parameters until you're satisfied with the alterations.

4. **After selecting and applying a filter or plug-in to an image or document, examine the result:**

An immediate update to your picture or file If you are dissatisfied with the results, you may reverse your modifications by selecting Edit Undo or reapplying the filter or plug-in.

Despite the fact that filters bring a great deal of diversity and interest to documents, they may quickly cause filter overload. Among the Creative Cloud apps, there are a variety of methods to apply filters, and certain approaches (and even the filters themselves) are regarded as superior to others.

Experiment freely with filters, but when constructing a final product, avoid using too many filters on a single portion of a picture. For instance, if you bevel and emboss a certain letter in many ways, that letter may become unreadable. Adding a substantial drop shadow may also divert the reader's attention away from other text elements.

Before generating your document, you should be aware of its intended purpose. If you start out to construct a project with a certain design in mind, you may obtain greater outcomes. Try sketching your ideas on paper, jotting down notes on the desired impact, and pondering the plug-ins you'll need to realize them. Use one filter at a time, and make sure the results are satisfactory before proceeding. If you are unsure of the desired impact or how to accomplish it, the option is to continue adding filters until you obtain the desired outcome.

Importing and Exporting Files

Because the tools in Creative Cloud work so well together, you will be copying, pasting, importing, and exporting content all the time between applications.

Importable and exportable content includes photos, text, word documents, and 3D objects, among others. You may discover that exporting files is necessary for other apps to recognize them.

If you save your files in the correct format, even non-Adobe apps will recognize your Creative Cloud application files. This chapter explains how to move files into and out of your different programs, beginning with Adobe Bridge, a standalone tool that comes with the Creative Cloud.

Learning About the Adobe Bridge Program

Adobe Bridge lets you organize and manage your assets, including images, text, video, and audio files, as well as those from non-Adobe programs such as Microsoft Word and Excel.

If you choose to access files through the Bridge interface, you can quickly move through folders and see thumbnails of files, as shown in Figure 5-1. You can also use the Filter tab to find files and look at their metadata, which may include keywords and information about copyright.

Bridge not only makes a vast amount of knowledge available, but it can also serve as a primary resource for all your help requirements.

Adobe Bridge may not be installed by default on your machine. The first time you access it from another program, the Adobe Application Manager will start and prompt you to install it.

Using the Bridge application

Whether or not Adobe Bridge is installed, you may still pick File Browse in Bridge from the majority of Creative Cloud apps. Choose Browse in Bridge to start Bridge or the Adobe Application Manager.

Choose FileBrowse in Mini Bridge to get to the Mini Bridge panel at the bottom of Photoshop's Essentials workspace. Figure 5-2 depicts Mini Bridge, which is simply a tiny version of Adobe Bridge.

Using Adobe Bridge to navigate

To move through Bridge, click the Folders panel in the upper left corner and choose the folder you want to look at.Find out how previews are made and how the icon for the default file type is changed automatically.

Be patient, as Adobe Bridge may take some time to generate the preview the first time you use it. To save this data or free up disk space, use ToolsCacheBuild and Export Cache or ToolsCachePurge Cache.

Choose a single file by double-clicking it, or

multiple files by Ctrl-clicking (Windows) or -clicking (Mac).With one or more files chosen, it is possible to

❖ Move the files to a new location by dragging them to a folder in the upper-left Folders panel. Use Bridge as the primary filing system. With the commands on the File menu, you may create new folders, remove or relocate files or file groups, and create new folders.

❖ The metadata panel is located in the lower-right

corner. Important camera data (EXIF) information, such as camera, flash, and f-stop, is included in the metadata. See Figure 5-3.

❖ Click the pencil icon in Figure 5-4 to add custom metadata to any item.

Pencil icon

❖ Use the Keywords
panel, seen in
Figure 5-5, to insert
your own keywords
that will assist you
in finding your
photographs later.

❖ Choose Edit-Find
or use the Filter
panel to find your
files in Bridge by
adding keywords,
descriptions, the
date they were
created, and other
criteria.

❖ Construct picture stacks. You may select numerous files in Bridge by selecting multiple files while holding down the Ctrl (Windows) or (Mac) key.

Next, select StackGroup as a stack by pressing Ctrl+G (Windows) or +G (Mac OS X) (Mac).As seen in Figures 5–6, it stacks the photos into a single thumbnail.

The number of pictures in the stack is shown in the image stack's upper-left corner.

Click the stack number to reopen the stack; click the stack number again to shut the stack. Choose StackUngroup from Stack or use the keyboard shortcut Ctrl+Shift+G (Windows) or +Shift+G (Mac OS X) (Mac).

Managing color

Using Bridge for color control saves time and increases output! Adobe Bridge allows you to alter the color settings for all Creative Cloud apps. Use Adobe Bridge's synchronized color management capabilities to provide color selections that are consistent across all Creative Cloud apps.

Select Modify Color Settings to choose a color management option that is uniform across all Creative Cloud apps, as seen in Figures 5-7.

Figure 5-7 depicts Joe's Press in a setting built using Adobe Photoshop. If your printer can provide you with the Joe's Press color settings, you can load them using the Color Settings dialog box in Photoshop and then make

them available to all of your CC programs by choosing them in Adobe Bridge.

Including Files inside a Document

Importing files is the same regardless of the application you're using. Some programs place a greater emphasis on the importation of material than others.

A piece of software like InDesign is dependent on

importing material into a document, which is then integrated into a page layout. Importing material is far less crucial in tools like Photoshop, since you typically begin modifying a picture that you open in Photoshop. In the sections that follow, we examine how to import material into each software program.

Inserting material into InDesign

Most of the time, you have to import pictures and text into InDesign to make a layout. You may pick text or graphic files from your hard drive or network when you select FilePlace. You can also choose audio and video files to use in making PDF documents for electronic distribution. After you choose a file to import, a preview of your image appears as a new cursor icon. This preview appears when the cursor is placed over the page or pasteboard. Place the imported content by clicking on the page where the image's upper-left corner should appear.

When you import different kinds of images, the Place dialog box pops up. From there, you can choose from a number of different ways to import the images.

To see more settings, you must check the box in the

Place dialog that says "Show Import Options." In Figures 5-8, you see the additional options that appear when an image is placed.

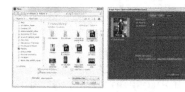

Choose FilePlace, and then choose a file to import. Check the option next to "Display Import Options," then click the "Open" button. The Image Import Options dialog box displays, with settings related to the image type being imported. For instance, if you are importing a bitmap picture (such as a JPEG), you may specify how the bitmap will look, whether it has a backdrop or color management information, and other settings.

When you import text information, you might lose some of the way the text was laid out in the original file. InDesign does not import anything it does not recognize into the document. Column and margin information is also frequently lost when text is imported. Nevertheless, certain available plug-ins help mitigate the issue to some degree.

The Launch Bridge button in the middle of the application bar in InDesign may be used to launch Adobe Bridge. Then, just drag and drop the desired photographs right from Bridge.

Content addition to a Photoshop file

You may either open a picture to work with or import stuff into an existing open project in Photoshop. Choose FilePlace in order to import AI, EPS, PDP, or PDF files. As illustrated in Figure 5-9, these files import into a new layer in the document, and you can then utilize tools to alter the imported material.

Your inserted Illustrator work is automatically incorporated into the Photoshop file. Double-click the layer containing the inserted artwork to access and modify the associated Illustrator file.

After saving the file, Photoshop instantly reflects the modifications. Notice that the original file has not been altered. Select FileGet Images from Camera to import images directly from your digital camera into Adobe Bridge.

Putting files into Illustrator

Illustrator allows the insertion of pictures and other types of data into a new document. By selecting FilePlace, you may upload Photoshop, PDF, image, and vector files. The Put dialog box will pop up, allowing you to choose a file for import.

Click the Put button to import the file. An Import dialogue box may appear at this point, depending on the type of file being imported. This dialog box provides a variety of choices for importing information into Illustrator. When importing a file containing layers, you may occasionally select between flattening the layers or maintaining them.

Encapsulated PostScript (EPS) is a file format that is often used for vector graphics, but it can also be used for other types of files.

Since many apps use this file format, you can obtain these files from other people. To import an EPS file, you must also choose FilePlace; after importing an EPS file into Illustrator, the file is transformed into Illustrator objects but cannot be edited. Choose FileOpen to edit the EPS object, or click the Edit

Original option in the Links window.

Illustrator can also import text documents. Illustrator supports Microsoft Word, TXT (text only), RTF (rich text format), and Unicode text documents, among others, and you may import them by selecting FilePlace. While importing a text file, you may be asked to choose the text's character set.

You may import files with the Put command, as well as copy and paste from other apps. You may copy a portion of a picture from Photoshop by hitting Ctrl+C (Windows) or +C (Mac) and then paste it into the Illustrator project.

Use the Put command whenever feasible to import material without degrading its quality. Additionally, transparency is not supported when copying and pasting from one program to another, but it is while using Put.

When certain plug-ins are installed, Illustrator may be able to import CAD files and other file types.

Enhancing Acrobat

Adobe Acrobat is mostly used to share finished documents. Most document creation and editing is done in other programs, like InDesign and Illustrator. But you may import a variety of data types into PDF files, and you can also do some creative things when placing data in PDF files:

❖ Comments made using Adobe Acrobat's review and markup tools are the most frequent and useful objects to import into an Adobe PDF file .By integrating comments into a PDF file, recommendations and input from several reviewers (people updating a document) may be consolidated into a single document. This feature facilitates the review process when several people are collaborating on a single document. To import comments into a PDF, click the Comment button, then, from the Comments List section, click the panel menu in the upper-right corner and choose Import Data File. When the Import Comments dialog box opens, go to the desired comment file and click Open.

If you are evaluating a

document, you can also choose Export All to Data File from the Remarks panel menu to export just the comments instead of sending the whole PDF file to the document owner.

❖ Form data: Choose Tools > Forms > Additional Form Options > Import Data to add form data to a PDF document. To import data, you can either export the form data from another PDF form or use a text file with spaces between the words. The data may then be shared across forms or with a database.

❖ Multimedia files: If you've ever desired to include a video or audio file in a PDF document, you're in luck. By clicking the Tools button, choosing Interactive Objects, and then clicking Add Video, Add Sound, or Add SWF, you can choose where the file should appear on the page and then choose whether to embed the multimedia file (compatible with Acrobat 6 and later) or create a link to the file (compatible with Acrobat 5 and earlier).

❖ Buttons: Adding buttons to flip pages, print a document, or visit a website makes your PDF files more user-friendly. Adding custom button images, like arrows or a printer symbol, makes your work stand out. Use the Button tool, which you can find by going to ToolsInteractive ObjectsAdd Button,

to place the button, and then choose the image file you want to use for the button's image. The picture file must be converted to PDF format beforehand.

❖ Preflight information: If you're sending a PDF file to a commercial printer for reproduction, you may want to preflight the file to verify that it fits the printer's requirements and has all the essential assets (such as fonts and pictures) for accurate printing. If your printer has provided a preflight profile for Acrobat, you may import it to guarantee that Acrobat checks for the items your printer has requested, such as certain font types and color standards. Import a preflight profile by selecting Tools—Print—Production—Preflight from the menu bar. In the resulting Preflight box, choose Options>Import Preflight Profile. If the Production Tools panel is not visible, click View Tools—Print Production and select Preflight from the list of production tools.

Bringing in Dreamweaver

With Dreamweaver, you may import the following file types into a website you are creating:

❖ Insert photos and other media, such as Flash, Flash Paper, and Flash Video, by selecting the Insert option from the menu.

❖ Import exported XML and XHTML

documents from InDesign.

❖ Cut and paste a layered Photoshop file. Simply select EditCopy Merged and then paste the file into Dreamweaver. You may then optimize the picture for the web in the subsequent Image Preview box (see Figure 5–10). Choose your options, then click OK. (Optimal online image settings are discussed in Book IV, Chapter 10).

Your Document Extraction

It is important to be able to export content from Adobe Creative Cloud documents to other applications, make the work public, and be able to access it on different machines. Adobe Creative Cloud gives you the ability to export a work in many file formats.

There are occasionally other applications that support importable Adobe documents. Adobe Flash CC can import Illustrator

73

AI files, Photoshop PSD files, and PDF documents, among others.

InDesign exportation

With InDesign, you may export pages or a book in as many file formats as you like. Specifically, you may export layouts as PDF files, which anybody with the free Adobe Reader can read. InDesign can also export to EPS and JPG, among other image and vector formats. A document created in InDesign may also be exported to SVG (Scalable Vector Graphics) and XML (Extensible Markup Language), which is handy when exporting for the web. InDesign provides a convenient tool for packaging your work for Dreamweaver.

By choosing FileExport in Dreamweaver, you can export the project you are currently working on and get it ready for page development.

If you pick FileExport and examine the Save as Type drop-down menu, you will notice a huge number of export possibilities, such as EPUB and HTML5. To learn more about these characteristics, see Chapter 8 of Book II.

Adobe Photoshop exporting material

If you work in the creative industry, you will export Adobe Photoshop files in many different formats, from simple.png or.jpg files to more complicated sliced pictures exported with HTML and CSS information. If you are interested in 3D and video, you will be pleased to learn that you can also export to a variety of video and 3D formats. Further detailed instructions may be found in Book IV.

Keep in mind that if you're working inside the Creative Cloud programs, you probably won't need to export any files since the majority of them recognize the native .psd format. For example, InDesign and Illustrator can both read paths and masks from a Photoshop document.

Transferring an Illustrator file

Illustrator enables exporting to a wide variety of file types. Several picture formats are available for exporting files. The Export dialog box appears when you choose File > Export. Click the Save As type (Windows) or Format (Mac) drop-down menu to examine the exportable file types.

After selecting a file format to export to, a second dialogue box may open, enabling you to choose from a variety of options for the exported file.

When exporting a file, try selecting the Flash SWF file format. A second dialog box with several choices, such as options to build an HTML page, save each layer as a distinct SWF document, and retain editability, appears (when possible). The choices accessible when exporting a document depend on the kind of file format you're exporting to.

Exporting Acrobat content

You can export parts of a PDF file that you are currently editing with Acrobat. In one of your files, for instance, you may use form data—the information that is entered into a form with text fields, etc. You may export this information from Acrobat and then transmit it online, which is useful given that PDF files are often too big for the web. As a result, only a small amount of prepared data is sent online, rather than a large PDF file. Moreover, portions of an Acrobat document may be exported for use in other applications.

You can export comments in a PDF to the Microsoft Word file that was used to make the PDF by clicking the Comment button and the panel menu in the Comments List area in the upper right corner, then choosing Export to Word. It is also possible to export comments to an AutoCAD file (if AutoCAD was used to make the PDF).In both cases, the original document that was used to make the PDF file must be present for the comments to be imported correctly.

Content exported from Dreamweaver

You can export your websites from Dreamweaver so that they are ready to be published and can be put on a live website. The site you're working on in Dreamweaver is exported to your hard disk prior to being uploaded to a server. The HTML styles used on a site you are developing may be exported and stored as an XML document, which can then be reused as needed. Afterwards, you may import these files into another Dreamweaver project you're working on. You may also use

FileConvert to convert your Dreamweaver file to other forms of HTML.

Handling Graphics, Paths, Text, and Fonts

Images, paths, text, and fonts are key components of Adobe Creative Cloud document creation. You must understand how to manage each aspect of your papers and make them work effectively together.The enjoyable part is discovering the many ways you may manipulate photos, text, and drawings.

You can use these features alone or together, and you'll probably learn something new each time you do.In addition to text, photos, and drawings, a layout may include other elements. In addition to text, photographs, and graphics, you may be dealing with music, animation, and video when you create documents for the web or PDF (Portable Document Format) files containing multimedia features.

Using Images in Your Papers

Graphics may be images, drawings, or vector objects. You can physically make graphics by creating markings on paper, or you may generate them digitally using software.

Graphics may be shown in several ways, including on a computer screen, projected onto a wall, or printed in a magazine or book.

Depending on how they are made digitally, computer graphics come in a variety of forms. Several processes are used to create bitmap and vector graphics for usage in your publications.

Using bitmap images

Bitmap graphics consist of numerous small squares, or "bits," arranged on an invisible grid. Depending on where and how the colors are organized on the grid, the image is produced when these dots are next to each other. If you zoom in close enough, you can even see the pixels that comprise the picture. With a 400% magnification, the picture in Figure 6-1 is composed of large squares. Nevertheless, when viewing the majority of bitmap pictures at their actual sizes, no pixels are visible.

Bitmaps are handy for displaying photos and applying text effects.

While painting or creating intricate visuals, bitmaps are widely used. But keep in mind that photographs might lose quality when they are scaled (their sizes are changed). As pixels are resized, the picture loses clarity and quality.

The majority of issues arise when a picture is magnified. Bitmap file types include PNG, BMP, GIF, JPG, PICT, and TIFF. Thankfully, Photoshop CC's enhanced upscaling tools allow you to maintain the picture quality required for a decent image.

Learning about vector graphics

Vector images (or graphics or drawings) vary significantly from bitmap images. A vector picture is produced using a sequence of mathematical calculations or code that specifies the image's formation. These computations instruct the computer on how to display and draw the lines on the page. Vector graphics are supported by the file extensions.eps,.ai,.pdf,.psd , and.svg.

Vector images often have smaller file sizes than bitmap graphics because the mathematical information necessary to construct the vector picture is typically less in file size than the information required to create each pixel in a bitmap. (Compression may reduce the file size of a bitmap, but the image is often bigger and slower to show.)

Due to this and the fact that vectors provide picture scaling, as seen in Figure 6-2, these images are well-suited for the web.

Scaling is simple with vectors since the algorithm just has to make minor adjustments to the computations to make the picture bigger or smaller. This implies that the file size will not vary, and the scaling will be extremely fast. The picture on a web page may be scaled to fill the browser window, regardless of its size, or made enormous for a banner. There is no degradation in quality, and the file size stays the same.

Choose FileSave if you wish to utilize vector graphics in your websites and apps. You may name your graphic and choose

SVG from the Save As Type drop-down option in the Save As dialog box.

Using Paths and Strokes

In a document, paths are the vector lines and outlines you construct. Paths may be used to outline an image, divide words, or be included in an artwork. Typically, you create routes using the Line tool, Pen tool, or form tools. These tools allow you to design trails of various widths and forms. You may also utilize tools to change the color and size of strokes (the lines that comprise a route).

Paths may be used to produce clipping paths and text paths. Clipping paths are used to mask (or conceal) page components. You define this mask using paths to construct a shape for the region you want to conceal. Even clipping routes may be exported to a file and imported into a new design pattern. Often, a picture with a clipping path is created in Photoshop CC and then imported into InDesign. Since InDesign can comprehend the clipping path, the desired masking region may be removed automatically.

When you wish to create text that flows along a route, you must first build a new path and then use the Type on a Path tool to write directly on the path. In Illustrator, for example, you build a path with the Pen tool and then pick the Type on a Path tool from the Tools panel. If you click the tool along the route you've established, you may enter new text along it.

If you have an existing route chosen, you may use the Type tool to traverse it. As illustrated in Figure 6-3, the type tool cursor changes to indicate that it is loaded as the type on a path tool. When you click

on the path, the type is associated with it.

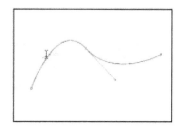

A stroke is the color, width, and style of the line used to build a route. Using the Pen tool, you may draw a line, and the line that makes up that route is the stroke. Still, this route may not have a stroke (shown by a diagonal line in the Tools, Swatches, and Stroke & Color panels), which means that the path itself is not visible. Figure 6-4 shows how the stroke (the outline) could be filled with a color or pattern.

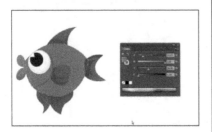

With Illustrator and InDesign, you may modify the color, width, style (or type), and form of a stroke using the settings and tools in the Tools panel and Stroke panel. You can also make big or small designs with strokes that are dashed or solid but have different widths. Figure 6-5 depicts several strokes.

Include Text

You may use text in your projects for several purposes. Text is commonly employed to teach and instruct readers, and this kind of publication is vastly distinct from those that use language solely for creative objectives. For instance, if you are writing an essay, you may position the content in columns underneath a prominent headline at the top of the page. On occasion, you may use text as a creative element or even as an object in place of a letter. Or, you may be building up a web page and utilizing the text for both a creative element in an animation and the content on web sites.

You may add text to a document using the Text tool or by importing text from Microsoft Word or another source. With a text field, you may enter a single line of text or enormous blocks of text with or without columns.

Text may be rotated and scaled, and its color, font face, orientation, and character size can be modified. Text may also be put on a path, as briefly discussed in the section under "Working with Paths and Strokes." You may then add text to your papers in an alternative manner by drawing a route and having the text follow it. Pathways are especially handy for page headers, footers, and artworks that use text as an aspect.

Use of typefaces

A font is the typeface of a collection of characters. You may change the font size to a variety of values, including the minuscule size 2 and the enormous size 200. There are names for fonts, such as Times New Roman and Comic Sans.

You may also encounter the term "glyph," which is a kind of character. The letter S is a glyph. Fonts are composed of glyphs. With Illustrator, you may examine glyphs in the Glyph panel (WindowTypeGlyphs). This is particularly handy when working with typefaces like Wingdings, which are composed of images rather than letters and numbers.

Your choice of typefaces can have a big effect on how your papers look, how they feel, and how they are written. Whether you're developing a layout for a magazine article or a digital work of art, the typefaces you choose affect the mood of your work. There are two primary classifications of typefaces, as seen in Figure 6-6:

❖ Serif: Each character has a little ornamental line at the beginning or end of each stroke.

❖ A character is sans-serif if it lacks tiny serifs.

Serif **Sans-serif**

Serif fonts can look older, more formal, or more literary, while sans-serif fonts look more modern. Obviously, this topic is entirely subjective. Examine the use of text on the Internet and in books, magazines, advertisements, and even newspapers. The manner in which text is typically employed has a significant impact on how others perceive your work and how it reads overall.

Finding an appropriate font can be a challenging but also enjoyable design task.

Learning about font kinds

Be mindful of the quality of your final output, despite the fact that you can get a trillion free fonts on the Internet. Professional graphic designers frequently use PostScript fonts, preferably OpenType fonts, which are more stable when printing than TrueType fonts, which may reflow when printing at different resolutions.

❖ TrueType: Similar to other digital font files, the TrueType font file includes information such as outlines, hinting instructions, and character mappings (which characters are included in the font). TrueType fonts are available in both Windows and Mac formats; however, the fonts developed for each operating system vary somewhat, so Windows and Mac users cannot exchange TrueType fonts.

❖ PostScript (Type 1): The scalable PostScript font system is compatible with PostScript printers; users may see fonts on the screen identically to how they would appear on paper. Type 1 font files include two files: a screen font with bitmap information for on-screen display and a file with outline information for printing. For high-quality printing, all components of the Type 1 font file (printer and screen fonts) must be included. Windows and Mac PostScript Type 1 fonts are not cross-platform compatible due to changes in their structures.

❖ OpenType: The OpenType font technology was developed by Adobe and Microsoft in collaboration. It is an expansion of the TrueType font system that can also store PostScript data. OpenType fonts are cross-platform, meaning that the same font file is compatible with both the Windows and Mac operating systems. This digital type format has expanded character sets and more sophisticated typographic settings. OpenType fonts include outline, metric, and bitmap information in a single file, similar to TrueType fonts. While any software that supports TrueType fonts may utilize OpenType fonts, not all non-Adobe products can access the full capabilities of the OpenType font system. In the font menus of a number of Creative Commons applications, you may discover the icons that symbolize the font type.

Using web-based text and typefaces

Sometimes, it is tough to use text and typefaces on the web. When fonts are used on a website, system fonts are utilized to display text. The fonts installed on the visitor's computer are often utilized to display the text.

The issue occurs if you use (or want to employ) fonts that are not installed on the visitor's PC. For instance, if you use the Papyrus font and the visitor does not have it, a new font is replaced, and the website seems entirely different.

Dreamweaver allows you to configure a collection of fonts to be used on each page while creating websites. Several typefaces are visually similar, and if one of them is unavailable, the following font is used instead.

At least one of the fonts in the set should be installed on the visitor's computer to guarantee that the layout of your web pages is preserved. With Photoshop and Illustrator, you may make a picture using any font available on your computer and then save it for the web. Select File > Save for Web.Dreamweaver may then be used to insert the picture on the web page. This option is ideal for little bits of text, such as buttons on a navigation bar, headers to divide sections of content, or a personalized banner at the top of a web page.

The Foundations of Page Design

Page layout combines the several components discussed previously in this chapter, mostly text and pictures (and sometimes other types of multimedia), to produce a page design. While designing a page, you must consider how people see the layout, such as how their eyes travel around the page to take in the information flow. Consider as well how the components are placed and how much space surrounds them.

This book discusses two primary types of page layout: print and web. Both formats require the use of several identical parts.

Selecting the Creative Cloud applications to utilize

There are some differences between making a layout for the web and making one for print, but you will find that you use a lot of the same tools and that a lot of the same information is used for both. Photoshop is commonly used to manipulate images for the web. In addition, it is the usual application for modifying and fixing pictures prepared for printing. With the Export XHTML/Dreamweaver function in InDesign, it is possible to create a page for both print and the web.

When posting information online, various precautions must be taken into account. Navigability, usability, file size, dimensions, and computer capabilities are web-specific problems that do not exist when designing for print. Nevertheless, quality, colors, and cropping (to mention a few) are factors to consider when creating a work for print that are not relevant to online design. Adobe Fireworks, which is included in Creative Cloud, is another alternative for designing web page layouts.

Fireworks not only aids in the creation of online visuals but also provides outstanding web prototyping capabilities. With Fireworks, you may set styles, create a master page, and add interactivity to your web sites. With Fireworks, it is simple to create multiple-page, hypertext-enabled prototypes.

Creating a print design layout

While designing a page layout for printing, you must take the paper size and font into account. Occasionally, you build letterhead with specific aspects (the primary content) that vary from page to page while other elements (the remainder of the page) stay constant. You may also construct page layouts that act as templates for a book and employ certain components (such as bullets or sidebars) in a variety of different ways across the pages. Printing requires careful consideration of page size, font size, and picture quality.

Image resolution is measured in pixels per inch (ppi), which refers to the number of pixels that are contained inside 1 inch onscreen. The printed resolution of an image is measured in dots per inch (dpi), with one dot of ink for each pixel. A picture with a higher dpi is crisper and contains finer details, which is crucial for printing. Printed photographs nearly always use a higher resolution than on-screen images; thus, you may discover that a 4-by-4-inch image on-screen (at 72 ppi) prints at less than 1-by-1 inch (at 300 dpi).

There are accessible templates for page layouts that account for standard paper dimensions and allow you to organize material into distinct sections. There are several types of templates accessible online, and you may occasionally download them for free; some are available for a little or moderate price, depending on the template. For instance, while designing a brochure, you may need to consider where the page will be folded and how to orient pictures and text so that they face the right direction when the brochure is being read. While designing a page layout, consider the following factors:

❖ Whenever feasible, use a grid and snap-to-align pieces. If specific items on your website are not aligned, there must be a valid cause.

❖ The eye follows the path of the components on the page. For instance, if a photograph of a person is facing away from the center of a spread, the viewer's gaze is drawn in that direction. Ensure that attention is drawn to the essential parts of the page.

❖ Follow a grid. Using a layout grid may help you arrange your information, whether you're preparing a printed or online article, even if it's not required. Please visit www.thegridsystem .org for additional information about grids.

Selecting a web page format

Web layout and print layout are very different. Nonetheless, many of the same difficulties exist in both print and digital layout, including making content readable and ensuring that it flows intelligently throughout the page (or screen). While designing a website, navigation and usability in web layouts open the door to a variety of considerations.

❖ Usability: A site that is usable is available to most, if not all, visitors. Visitors must be able to quickly access your material because the writing is readable, the file formats are compatible with their machines, and the information is easily discoverable. Additionally, visitors with physical disabilities, such as vision or reading difficulties, may utilize software to have the website read or spoken aloud to them.

❖ The best method to construct a good site is through extensive planning and drawing. If it has been a while since you've used a pencil and sketchbook, make it a habit to always have both on hand. By noting the demands of the average user, you may establish which information on the page must be the most accessible and conspicuous. The next step is to begin sketching out your thoughts. Sketching helps you iterate (create new versions) repeatedly without feeling committed to a single concept. Determine the site's user experience before you begin constructing pages. You will not only save days but also have a far more successful website.

❖ Size: File size should always be kept to a minimum, which may necessitate modifying your layout's dimensions. If several components of your design need huge photos, you may need to entirely alter the design to lower the file size. Additionally, you must design the page with the typical user's monitor in mind. If the width of your website exceeds 780 pixels, it will scroll horizontally on a visitor's monitor with a resolution of 800 by 600. While developing websites, you must consider the dimensions of visitors' displays to avoid annoying the majority of users.

- ❖ There are now a variety of methods for automatically scaling and rearranging material. Study Book VI of Adobe Dreamweaver, specifically Chapter 8, to learn more about utilizing Cascading Style Sheets to dynamically adapt your website to user demands.
- ❖ Visitors must be able to traverse the pages of your website. To facilitate this, you

must construct linkages to these sites using buttons, text links, menus, and other graphical components. It requires considerable time and preparation to make navigational controls simple to locate and utilize. Ensure that navigation plays a significant role in the layout of your website.

You must consider not just usability and navigation but also the numerous types of devices that may access the website and how users from across the globe may attempt to access it. If you want your website to be accessible to everyone, you may need to translate it into many languages and use various character sets. (This also applies to print if you're creating a page that requires a different character set than you usually use.)

Since you may include multimedia (such as photos and animation) in addition to text, you must consider the dimensions and color constraints of the user's device as well as file size and scrolling.

Using Color

One of the most important things to think about

when making projects is how to use color in documents. The colors you use, the mode in which you use them, and even the manner in which you select colors affect the appearance of your artwork.

This document appears to be completed. You learn the fundamentals of how color affects the projects you're working on, as color is a vast topic. It is important to plan how you will use color, and the type of output you intend for the document will heavily influence this plan. Different color modes are suitable for on-screen graphics as opposed to those that are professionally printed.

You may be working with colors that a company requires to match its logo, or you may be creating an image that replicates how a building should be painted using specific colors of paint. Pantone colors, also known as PMS (Pantone Matching System) or color mixes, may be necessary, if not for the printing process then to match a client's color request.

You are introduced to color modes and their applications. In addition, you learn new terminology and how to locate, blend, and add colors to your documents in Creative Cloud.

Consideration of Color Modes and Channels

Within the Creative Cloud applications, multiple color modes are accessible. When you create a new document in Photoshop or Illustrator, you can choose the color mode to use. In fact, Photoshop and Illustrator allow you to select a color mode in the New Document dialog box. Your decision affects the way colors are created.

Later, go to FileDocument Color Mode in Illustrator or ImageMode in Photoshop to change the color mode. Generally, CMYK mode is employed when working with print. RGB is the format to use when creating files for display on a monitor.

Using RGB

RGB (Red, Green, Blue) is the color mode used for on-screen presentation, such as an image displayed on the web or a broadcast design for television. Each color displayed on-screen is comprised of a specific proportion of red, green, and blue (between 0% and 100%). In the Color panel, you can either set the level of values using sliders, as shown in Figure 7-1, or enter a percentage in a text field.

Observe the exclamation point on the color panel, which represents the out-of-gamut symbol. It indicates that the color cannot be reproduced accurately in CMYK mode. Click the CMYK warning exclamation point to convert to a color that is compatible with the CMYK gamut.

When you create a web page, the color is represented as a hexadecimal number consisting of three pairs of letters and numbers (A through F and 0 through 9)—the first pair for red, the second pair for green, and the last pair for blue. The smallest value (the smallest amount of the color) in a hexadecimal number is 0 (zero), while the largest value (the largest amount of the color) is F. Black is represented by #000000, white by #FFFFFF, red by #FF0000, and light gray by #CCCCCC. To see what a specific hexadecimal color looks like, go to Visibone at http://htmlcolorcodes.com/.

Utilization of CMYK

CMYK—Cyan, Magenta, Yellow, and Key (or Black)—is the standard color mode for print media, especially in commercial printing like that performed by a service provider.

The CMYK color scheme is based on pigment (a coloring substance) color separation and describes how light reflects off pigments. In this color mode, black is produced by combining the maximum cyan, magenta, and yellow values. By combining equal, but not maximum, amounts of cyan, magenta, and yellow, you can create different shades of gray. White is the total absence of color. However, Epson, Hewlett-Packard (HP), and Canon desktop printers use their own color systems to print your documents.

Gray scale cost savings

The pictures in this book were printed in grayscale, so you've seen a lot of black-and-white pictures that look like they were made in color. Gray scale refers to the various shades of gray that can be printed with only black ink on a white page. Halftone patterns are made when a picture uses dots of different sizes or a lot of small dots in the same spot to make it look like there are different shades of gray. Halftone patterns can look like different colors by adding dots to make shadows and color gradients.

Visualizing color channels

When working with an image in Photoshop, the image has at least one, but typically more than one, color channel. A color channel stores information about a particular color within an image. An RGB image, for instance, contains three color channels: one for reds (R), one for greens (G), and one for blues (B).

In addition to the three color channels, a picture may also include an alpha channel that stores transparency information. If you are using a file format that allows transparency, you may add and use the alpha channel to store alpha information. The file formats png, tiff, gif, dcs, eps, and the native ai and psd formats enable transparency.

You may also store a selection using an alpha channel. By selecting Save

Selection in Photoshop, you may save your selection to an alpha channel. You may reload your selection at any moment by selecting Select Load Selection and selecting the channel.

Choose WindowChannels to access the channels in your picture in Photoshop. While the Channels panel is shown, you may control the visibility of each icon by clicking the eye symbol that appears next to it. (Please see Figure 7-2.)

Selecting Colors

You may be limited in the number of colors you can use while creating a document or you may be able to use an infinite number of colors. If you prefer to print your papers, you may choose a particular palette of colors. A corporate logo may be limited to two colors, or you may be required to print in gray scale. Locating the colors you need to utilize in each software program is crucial, and learning how to access them frequently in a document can save you a great deal of time.

Using samples

A swatch is an effective way to choose a color, especially when printing a document. Among the different Creative Cloud applications, the Swatches panel includes colors and gradients. (Figure 7-3 depicts the Swatches panel from Illustrator.) You may construct libraries of color swatches that can be used again across several pages.

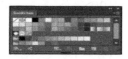

You may choose swatch libraries from the panel menu, as well as load and store swatch libraries. You can alter a swatch library by adding or removing colors.

Blending colors

The Color Panel has a color mixer that facilitates the selection of colors. You may choose a color by using the eyedropper tool or, if you prefer, by entering numbers or percentages for each hue. Many color options are available in the applications you use, giving you a great deal of freedom for all of your undertakings.

Follow the instructions below to choose a color in a certain color mode:

1. In an application with a color panel, choose WindowColor (if it's not currently open) to access the color panel. The Color panel is accessible in Photoshop,

InDesign, and Illustrator.

2. Choose a new color mode by clicking the Color Panel's menu.

   Click the arrow button in the upper-right corner of the Color Panel to access this menu.

3. Choose the RGB color mode from the opening panel menu.

   The display switches to RGB mode.

4. In the Color panel, select the desired color by clicking the Fill box (a solid square) or the Stroke box (a hollow square).

   Clicking the Fill box, you can change the color of a fill (the color within a shape).Clicking the Stroke box allows you to change the color of a stroke (the outline of a shape or a line).

5. Adjust the color values using the sliders in the Color Panel.

   Moreover, the percentage numbers to the right of each slider are modifiable.

6. After selecting an appropriate color,

return to your project and build a new shape using the color.

When you hold down the Shift key while altering a single color slider, the other color sliders will shift proportionately to give you multiple tints based on the original.

Color Use on the Web

In the past, you were forced to deliberately choose the colors you used on the web. Certain computer displays could only show a limited number of colors. Today's color monitors are far more sophisticated and can show a wide variety of hues, so online pictures are much more likely to appear accurately.

Despite the fact that this remark has nothing to do with color, Macintosh and Windows computers show your work differently due to gamma variances. In general, colors on a Mac seem lighter, while colors on a PC appear darker.

Despite the fact that most computers can handle a vast array of colors, you may need to consider color restrictions. If you are developing a website for older machines or a certain user base, you may be required to restrict colors to the 256 web-safe colors. This implies that any additional colors used will be approximated, which might result in an unattractive appearance. Consider the following if your site is likely to be accessed by people with older computers:

❖ When designing websites for older devices, use a web-safe palette of 216 colors so that you know how the pages will appear. This number is 216 as opposed to 256 since it is compatible with both Mac and Windows machines. This panel, often referred to as the "Web-Safe Palette" or "Web-Safe RGB," is accessible through the Swatches panel menu in Illustrator and Photoshop.

❖ Avoid utilizing gradients, if feasible. They employ a wide range of colors (many of which are not supported by a limited web panel).

❖ Avoid hesitating whenever possible. A color that is approximated because it cannot be handled by a computer is dithered; the computer attempts to utilize two or more colors to produce the color you selected, resulting in an unattractive grainy look. Hence, a small number of colors might have a detrimental influence on a picture; see the granular look of the face in Figure 7-4.

If you keep the previous list of suggestions in mind, you are ready to begin site design! Note that you do not need to worry about utilizing the web-safe color palette if you are mainly designing for modern PCs.

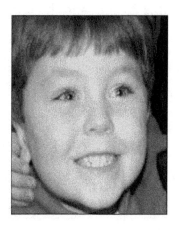

Printing Documents

The Adobe Creative Cloud programs provide a variety of printing options for documents. Similarly, you may print a variety of document types. You can produce anything from a 300-page book to an iron-on T-shirt transfer using the Creative Cloud's applications. You learn the sorts of printers you may use, what to purchase (and from whom) in order to utilize them, and how to save your work to increase the quality of the print job after you've completed it.

Selecting Printers

When it comes to printers, there are several alternatives available at a wide range of prices. Quality, cost of maintenance, and printing speed might vary significantly among printers. Some inkjet printers excel at printing full-color photographs but not text; a low-end or mid-range laser printer can produce black-and-white documents with high speed and clarity but cannot print in color.

Using home printers

Nowadays, the most prevalent form of consumer (home) printer is an inkjet printer, which operates by spraying ink from cartridges onto a sheet of paper as it goes through the printer. This sort of color printer is prevalent in homes since it is the least expensive option. It is also adaptable. You can get a color inkjet printer (which can print resumes, photographs, and brochures) for a reasonable price at practically any computer shop.

The only disadvantage of inkjet printers is that they might be costly to maintain over time. Depending on how often you print, you may need to frequently change the black or color cartridges, which may be expensive and rapidly surpass the printer's purchase price.

Considering skilled printers

Professional printers offer a more comprehensive feature set than consumer printers. Professional printers can be inkjet or laser printers, and they can serve a variety of functions in the workplace. Multi-function office printers are often referred to as "multifunction" or "all-in-one" printers and incorporate scanning, photocopying, and faxing in addition to printing. Small companies and home offices may benefit from these all-in-one units since they save the customer money and provide access to a range of valuable tools.

Laser printers often generate better-quality output, print pages more quickly than inkjet printers, and create documents with a clean, professional appearance. Also, you may print more pages per ink cartridge, saving money on consumables.

Purchasing a Printer

Common qualities to look for when choosing a printer (consumer or professional) include the following:

- ❖ Printer speed is measured in pages per minute (PPM). Low-end inkjet printers generally produce black-and-white pages at a rate of 12 or fewer pages per minute (PPM). While printing color documents, the number of pages per minute decreases.

- ❖ Color: Almost all inkjet printers can print in color, while many only print in monochrome.

Color printers may be costly to maintain since the majority of inkjet printers need two ink cartridges: one for black ink and one for colored ink. When one color runs out, you are required to change the complete cartridge; otherwise, none of the colors will print correctly. There are color laser printers available; however, they are often rather costly.

- ❖ Similar to displays, the quality of a printer may be measured by its resolution. A higher resolution makes pictures and text more distinct. Low-end or older inkjet printers may print at a maximum resolution of 600 dpi (dots per inch), which is enough for text but inadequate for printing images of good quality.

- ❖ Connectivity: There are three methods to connect a printer to a computer. Typically, older printers connect to your system through a parallel (36-pin) connector, but modern printers have both parallel and USB (Universal Serial Bus) ports. Connecting a printer to your network is the third method of connecting to a printer; however, this option is often reserved for professional printers.

- ❖ Duplexing: Another feature to consider is duplexing, the ability to print on both sides of a sheet of paper without manually flipping and reloading the page.

Publish your work

When it comes to printing, there are several choices and configurations that might affect the final outcome of your paper. Whether you are printing banners, business cards, T-shirt iron-on transfers, or lost-cat posters, you must consider various things, including paper quality, printer quality, and ink consumption. You must also choose whether you will print the papers at home or take them to a professional printing company.

While RGB (red, green, and blue) is the online color standard, CMYK (cyan, magenta, yellow, and black) is the print standard.

Selecting how and where to print

When it comes to printing your files, you have numerous alternatives available.

You can take your digital files to a printing service provider, which is a business that prints electronic documents (such as FedEx Office or office supply shops like Staples), or you can print the files on your inkjet or laser printer at home.

Each alternative has several benefits and drawbacks. Depending on the quantity of copies and the number of colors, it might be prohibitively expensive to have files professionally printed. Getting files printed by a professional print shop will almost always result in far higher print quality than if they were produced on a low-end inkjet printer.

Obviously, if you're merely printing flyers to distribute in your area, you may not need high-quality output, and a home inkjet or laser printer may suffice. But printing papers professionally may be more cost-effective than printing them at home if you need to use a lot of black ink or more than one or two toner cartridges.

While using an inkjet printer, you can typically print between 400 and 600 pages of black text before having to change a cartridge; a laser printer can print between 2,500 and 4,000 pages before requiring fresh toner.

Depending on the number of pages you need to print and if you need to print in color, utilizing a laser printer may save you hundreds of dollars every year. If you need to print in color, there are several color laser printers to choose from (although they can be expensive). Some entry-level color laser printers may cost under $500, while some high-end models can exceed $10,000.

Black-and-white laser printers may be purchased for as little as $100. So, unless you want to print several papers, outsourcing your printing may be the best option.

The kind of printer you employ (such as a business or PostScript printer or an inexpensive home inkjet) has a significant impact on the output quality. The majority of graphics and photos will appear much better when printed professionally.

Looking at paper

When printing your papers, choose the most appropriate sort of paper. If you want to print on glossy paper, ensure that the paper is compatible with your printer. While the majority of glossy paper is compatible with inkjet and laser printers, many brands and varieties may not.

Always double-check the paper you purchase to ensure that it will not harm your printer. The types of printers supported by the paper are listed on the package.

One advantage of glossy paper is that it has a similar finish to picture paper, which may make your printing look of greater quality. Utilizing quality paper may result in photographs with more vibrant colors and more detail. When selecting printer paper, the following properties are crucial to consider:

- ❖ Brightness refers to the brightness of the paper. Higher scores indicate that the paper seems whiter and cleaner.
- ❖ Weight refers to the density of the paper. The greater the weight, the thicker and more durable the paper.
- ❖ Opacity refers to the degree to which the paper is translucent or transparent. If the paper is too thin, too much light will flow through it; moreover, you may be able to see the ink through the opposite side of the page (this might be problematic if you want to print on both sides of the sheet). A heavier sheet of paper would be thicker and allow less light to travel through it

due to its greater opacity.

- ❖ Texture describes the smoothness or roughness of the paper's surface. Texture may differ significantly between inkjet and laser printers. Inkjet printers spray ink onto a page, so having a somewhat textured surface to print on might be advantageous since the roughness causes the ink to dry somewhat quicker and bleed less, resulting in a sharper-looking final output. In contrast, the reverse is true when utilizing a laser printer. If the toner is transferred onto a smooth, flat surface, the results are superior.

Note that you cannot always print on 8-1/2 by 11-inch (also known as letterhead or A4) paper. Many printers provide printing on envelopes, labels, stickers, business cards, and even iron-on transfers. You may build your own T-shirts with your company's logo or with your face on the front using iron-on transfers. Several modern printers permit printing directly onto the CD-ROM surface. Even tiny printers intended only for printing standard-sized images are available for purchase.

Furthermore, it is critical to note that paper sizes vary greatly. The United States and Canada measure paper in inches, but the rest of the world uses metric units based on an ISO (International Organization for Standardization) standard.

The ISO A4 format may replace the North American Letter format. The third distinction between the U.S. and Canadian systems and the ISO is that ISO paper sizes always adhere to a defined ratio, but the U.S. and Canadian systems use two different aspect ratios.

Storing files for an expert printer or service provider

Find out which file formats a professional printing business supports before dealing with them. Virtually all print service providers accept files made using Adobe software (Illustrator, Photoshop, InDesign, or Acrobat, for example) as well as files created with QuarkXPress, CorelDRAW, or other professional-level software. Verify the version and operating system that the service provider accepts, since you may be needed to save your files so that they are compatible with the version of software that the service provider employs.

If your service provider doesn't accept native InDesign or QuarkXPress files, you may need to convert your work to a universal file format, such as PDF (Portable Document Format). In reality, exporting as a PDF is the best option. When you produce a PDF (with the appropriate parameters), you effectively encapsulate everything necessary to print your work properly.

For the majority of your applications, pick FileExport or FileSave and choose PDF; if you are sending the output of InDesign or Illustrator to a professional printer, we suggest that you print to a PDF using the following steps:

1. As illustrated in Figure 8-1, pick FilePrint and then Postscript File from the Printer drop-down menu.

2. Choose Adobe PDF as the PPD format.

3. Choose Setup from the choices on the left side of the Print dialog box to get a preview of your

page art in the lower-left corner. (See Figure 8-1.)

4. Verify that your page art is properly positioned in the document window. If your artwork is positioned incorrectly, adjust it appropriately. If your document does not fit on the specified print size, choose Scale to Fit.

Preview window

5. Select marks and blemishes from the choices shown on the left. If necessary, enable crop markings and registration marks. To save your modifications as a PostScript file, click Save.

6. Start Adobe Distiller (included in Adobe Acrobat XI) and choose FileOpen to open your PostScript file. Use the Adobe Application Manager to identify and install Adobe Acrobat XI Pro from Creative Cloud if you are

lacking the complete Acrobat XI installation.

7. Choose Press Quality from the Default Settings drop-down menu for a high-resolution output, as shown in Figure 8-2

Distiller converts the file to PDF automatically, depending on the current parameters.

PDF printing is the industry standard

When you're ready to print a document, you can open the Print dialog box and choose from a variety of options based on the kind of printer you've installed. In this instance, Adobe PDF is used. While you may simply create a Photoshop PDF from the Save menu, we will guide you through the procedures for producing a PDF via the Print dialog box. With the Print dialog box, you may access extra choices that are not accessible via the Save menu, including the ability to preview printed documents, scale photos, and apply color adjustments.

Follow these instructions to print a file as a PDF from Photoshop CC:

1. Select File > Print. As illustrated in Figure 8-3, the Print Options dialog box appears.

2. In the Printer drop-down menu, choose Adobe PDF. You may also pick an installed printer here if you wish to configure its settings.

The Print dialog box differs depending on the software.
In this dialog box,

Photoshop enables you to modify the picture's scale by entering a number in the Scale text box or by choosing and dragging a handle on the image preview on the left.

3. Set the quality of your output now. Click the Print Settings button after selecting Adobe PDF as the printer. The supplementary Adobe PDF Document

Properties dialog box seems to be output-specific.

4. In this dialog box, seen in Figure 8-4, you may pick the desired PDF quality from the Default Settings drop-down menu.

5. (Optional) To see your PDF file immediately after it is prepared, choose View Adobe PDF Results. Click OK after leaving all other settings at their defaults. You are returned to the Print dialog box.

6. Ensure that color handling is set to "Printer Manages Color" under color management.

If you have a color management system in place, you should consult your IT professional.

7. Choose Normal Printing and Relative Colorimetric for Rendering Intent in Color Management.

8. Scroll down until you reach the position and size section. Use the Scale to Suit Media checkbox to scale the image to fit the media if necessary.

instructions on utilizing its capabilities.

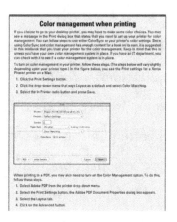

9. Click the print button.

   The Save As dialog box is shown.

10. Specify a name for the PDF, go to the desired place, and click Save.

    The file is stored in PDF format.

Due to the fact that most printers have unique interfaces for configuring settings, you may need to reference the printer's manual for specific

INTRODUCING INDESIGN CC

InDesign is a complex application for page layout. It may be used to generate publications with a professional appearance, such as newsletters, booklets, and magazines. You may also use it to produce papers for distribution on tablets like the iPad, as well as interactive or video-rich documents.

InDesign has grown into a program that can put content online or in print on almost any device. With InDesign, you can, for example, make a document and print it, add links and video, and turn it into PDF or HTML.

As sophisticated as InDesign is, you may expect it to be tough to use, but you'll discover that generating even the most basic pages is a breeze. This mini-guide demonstrates how to use InDesign to design innovative page layouts.

Starting off with InDesign CC

InDesign is used to create page layouts with text, graphics (such as fills and strokes), and photographs. Figure 1-1 shows an InDesign document with logos from Adobe Illustrator and images from Photoshop. If this file were exported as a PDF or HTML file, it might have video and buttons that you can click on.

In the following sections, you learn how to create and open documents with InDesign.

New publication creation

You may create a new InDesign document after launching the program. To start a new magazine, just follow these steps:

1. Go to File > New > Document.
   Figure 1-2 depicts the appearance of the New Document dialog box.

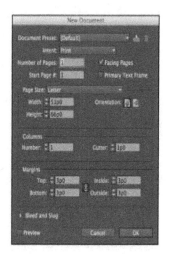

2. Choose if you are creating for print, online, or digital publishing.
   Document (digital) from the Intent drop-down menu.

Choose the Preview option at the bottom of the New Document window if you wish to get a preview of your edits in this panel. The changes you make in the subsequent stages will alter the look of the document in InDesign as you make your adjustments.

3. Insert a value in the "Number of Pages" text box to indicate the total number of pages in the document.

This number might range between 1 and 9999. Make an educated estimate as to the number of pages in your manuscript if you are uncertain. With the Pages panel, you may simply add pages in the future.

4. Select the Facing Pages checkbox to arrange the pages as spreads with left and right pages for this example.

With this option chosen, the pages of your document are grouped in pairs, resulting in "spreads," which are two facing or neighboring pages in a layout. For instance, if you are developing a publication that will be formatted as a book or magazine, you would pick this option. If you reject this option, pages will be ordered independently,

which is ideal for a single-page flyer or a document with just front and back sides.

5. Choose a page size from the drop-down menu labeled "Page Size."

The page size should be set to the size of the paper that will be used for printing or the size of the material that will be shown. Depending on the selected size, the width and height values appear below this drop-down menu.

You may also build a custom size by entering your own values. Depending on the values entered in the Width and Height sections of the Page Size section, the Orientation option changes from portrait (tall) to landscape (wide).

The options in the Page Size drop-down menu are

determined by your selection of intent. If you pick Web for the Intent, you may select from several screen resolutions; however, if you select Digital Publication, you can select from common tablet sizes, such as those of the iPad, NOOK/Kindle Fire, and Android.

You may input page sizes using the most prevalent units of measurement, or you can just use the relevant abbreviation. You would type "8" for 8 inches and "15 cm" for 15 centimeters. You may utilize the majority of units of measurement in all InDesign dialog boxes and panels; just select the unit of measurement you want to use. These values are converted to pixels when making online or digital documents.

6. Determine the number of columns on the page.

This stage generates column guides for non-printing or non-displaying columns.

Finished project these instructions will assist you in organizing your pages as you build them. Also, you may specify a number in the Gutter box, which determines the distance between each column.

7. Select the page's margin settings.

See the "Make All Settings the Same button, represented by a chain, in the center of the four text fields where you input margin values. Toggle this button to set all margins to the same value (a solid chain icon) or to set them to different values (a broken chain icon).

If you see Top, Bottom, Inside and Outside, you are choosing margins for a page layout with facing pages, which was previously selected. When you see Top, Bottom, Left, and Right, you're building a page layout with pages that don't face each other. The inner margins refer to the margins in the center of the spread, while the outside margins refer to the margins on the left and right sides of a book or magazine. To fit the binding of a book, which may need broader margins than the exterior, you may adjust the inside setting.

If you use the same settings often, it is advisable to save them as a preset. Click the Save Document Preset button, which is situated to the right of the Document Preset drop-down menu in the New Document dialog box, before clicking OK. Provide a name for the preset, then press the OK button. Whenever you create a new document, you can then pick settings from the Document Preset drop-down list (see the top of Figure 1-2).

8. Click OK when you are done.

After clicking OK in the Create Document dialog box, a new document with the selected parameters is generated.

Opening an existing publication

On your hard drive, you may have InDesign files that you have generated or saved from another source. To open existing InDesign documents (files with the extension.indd), follow these steps:

1. Click FileOpen.
   The Open dialog box appears.
2. Browse your hard drive and open a file of your choice.
   To choose a file, click the file's title.
   To select several files, use Ctrl (on a Mac) while clicking the filenames.

3. Click the Open button to access a file.
   The file opens inside the current workspace.

Considering the document layout

If you need to modify the page size or page count of a document that is already open in the workspace, you may do it in the Document Setup dialog box. To view and edit Document Setup dialog box settings, follow these steps:

1. Choose File > Document Setup.

Opens the Document Setup dialog box.

Note: If you require the number of pages in your document to be larger or smaller than the current figure, you may adjust the value in the Number of Pages text area. After closing this dialog box, the page count of your document will be updated. In addition to the Pages panel, you can add more pages by selecting LayoutPagesInsert Pages to insert several pages or LayoutPagesAdd Page to add a single page.

2. To alter the page size, choose a new option from the Page Size drop-down menu or manually enter numbers into the Width and Height text boxes. You may also choose a new value by using the up and down arrows in the Width and Height text sections.

3. Click the Portrait or Landscape button to alter the orientation of the page.

After closing this dialog box, the page orientation is updated in the workspace.

4. Click OK after you have completed modifying the document's settings.

The changes are applied to the document that is now open.

If you modify the Document Setup dialogue box while no documents are open, the changes become the default settings for all new documents you create.

Observing the Workplace

Like the other Creative Cloud products, InDesign has a common layout. With dockable panels and a single-row Tools panel, you can free up much more space in your workspace.

The workspace, or user interface, of InDesign has a huge variety of tools and panels, yet the majority of users only use a handful. You will likely use many panels repeatedly, so you should make them readily accessible. Several of these panels are already docked on the right in the default user workspace. Figure 1-1 depicts the InDesign workspace layout when a new document is opened. The Windows workspace of InDesign is substantially similar to that of the Macintosh version.

The following items compose the InDesign workspace:

❖ The primary section of the InDesign workspace is a page. It is the region that is printed or exported after a layout is complete.

❖ Master pages: With a master page, you may specify how certain text components and pictures look across a whole document (or just sections of it). It is similar to a template for your document in that you may reuse components across pages. For instance, if you want a certain element to appear on each page (such as page numbering), you may add it to the master page. If you need to modify an element on the master page, you may do it at any time, and the changes will be reflected on all pages where the master page has been applied. Master pages are accessible via the Pages panel.

❖ A "spread" is a collection of two or more pages that will be printed side by side. As you open periodicals and books, you often see spreads, just like the book you are now holding. If your project has a single page, you will not see a spread in the InDesign document window. If you decrease the magnification, InDesign will show just one page or, if the page is two-sided, both sides.

❖ Pasteboard: The pasteboard is the region around a page's margins. You may utilize the pasteboard to temporarily store things before incorporating them into your layout. There is no sharing of pasteboards across pages or spreads. For instance, if you have set specific items on a pasteboard for pages 4 and 5, you cannot access them while working on pages 8 and 9; hence, each page or spread has its own pasteboard.

Tools

The Tools panel contains tools for editing, manipulating, and selecting document objects as well as capabilities for making page alterations. To choose a tool, just use the mouse and click on it. Figure 1-4 depicts the default configuration of the Tools panel.

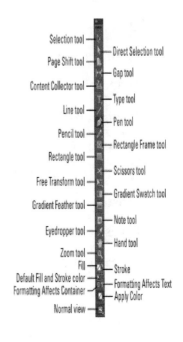

If you decide that a single row of tools is not for you, you may return to an earlier version of the Tools panel by clicking the two arrows on the gray bar at the panel's top. To reposition the tools, click the bar at the top of the tools, under the double arrows, and drag the panel to a new spot.

Using the tools in the Tools panel, the following can be accomplished:

- ❖ Create awe-inspiring new content on a page using the drawing, text, and frame tools.
- ❖ Select existing page content to move or modify.
- ❖ View the page in a variety of ways by panning and zooming the page or spreading.
- ❖ Modify pre-existing objects, including shapes, lines, and text. Utilize the selection tool to select existing objects for modification.

A small arrow next to a tool's icon indicates that there are other tools behind it. When you click the tool and hold down the mouse button, a menu of additional tools will appear. Move the cursor to the tool you want to use while holding down the mouse button. Let go of the button when the tool is highlighted.

Menus

With the menus on the main menu bar, you can access some of InDesign's most important commands and change how the program looks. You can also use them to open and close panels that let you edit and set up the publication.

Most of the InDesign menu commands, including New, Open, and Save, are likely familiar to you from other applications. InDesign's menus also have commands like "Insert with Placeholder Text" that are used only for page layout.

The following choices are available through the InDesign main menu:

❖ File: Some of the most important options for making, opening, and saving documents are on this menu. It also has the Put command, which lets you add new information, and several options for controlling document settings, exporting documents, and printing.

❖ Edit: This menu gives you access to many commands for editing and managing selections, like copying and shortcuts for the keyboard. The dictionary and spell checker are also accessible from this menu.

❖ Use the Layout menu to create guides. These options allow you to accurately position and align elements on the page. Utilize the menu to navigate the pages and spreads of the document.

❖ Type: This menu allows you to select fonts and control layout characters. You can access the numerous text-related settings via

this menu, which opens the associated panel where changes are made.

❖ With this menu, you can change how things look and where they are on the page.The choices on this menu depend on what part of the workspace you have chosen, like a text field or an image.

❖ Table: This menu lets you set up, change, and manage the tables on the page.

❖ View: From this menu, you can modify the page's

view, including zooming in and out, and work with guides, rulers, and grids to help you arrange elements.

❖ Window: Use this menu to toggle between open documents or to open and close panels.

❖ Help: From this menu, you can access the InDesign help documents and configure any installed plug-ins.

Panels

The document is displayed in a large area in the default layout. Some panels snap to the edge of the workspace to the right of the document; panels that are connected to the edge of the workspace are called docked. Panels are used to manage publishing and alter page components. It is possible to maximize, decrease, reposition, and shut panels.

Just clicking a panel's name will cause it to expand. When a different panel is chosen, the expanded panels are immediately compacted again.

To work with all panels enlarged, click the twin left-pointing arrows on the gray bar above the panels. You can hide all the panels by clicking the two arrows pointing to the right on the gray bar above the larger panels.

Even though some InDesign panels do different things, panels that do similar things are put together based on what they do. You may alter the categories by dragging the tab of a panel into a different grouping.

Some panels on an InDesign page change when different types of content are changed. For the time being, we will quickly introduce you to the Control and Pages panels of InDesign.

Control panel

As shown in Figure 1-5 for the Type tool, the Control panel, which is located across the top of the document window, is used to modify virtually any element you have selected in InDesign. This panel responds to what you have chosen on the page, so its contents change depending on what you have chosen. For instance, if you have selected text within a page frame, the Control Panel will display options for editing the text. If a shape is selected, the panel will display options for modifying the shape.

The Control Panel is depicted in Figures 1–6 when a frame is selected using the Selecting device. The Control Panel menu allows for the selection of frame options.

Pages panel

The Pages panel allows you to manage pages, as shown in Figure 1–7. This panel allows you to rearrange, add, and delete document pages. You can use the Pages panel to create alternative layouts for vertical and horizontal displays on a tablet when creating electronic documents.

You can also add and delete pages by selecting Layout Pages or by using the keyboard shortcut Ctrl+Shift+P (Windows) or +Shift+P to add pages (Mac).

You can hide all open panels, including the Control panel, by pressing.

Tab key; press Tab to bring them back into view. You can leave tools and panels hidden in InDesign CC and reveal them by moving the cursor to the left or right side of the work area. As you hover over the narrow vertical gray bar on either side of the workspace, the tools or panels (depending on which side you're on) will return! Also, they disappear after you leave the location.

You may navigate the document's pages using the left and right arrow buttons to the left and right of the page number in the lower-left corner of the window. You may also navigate to a particular page by entering a page number and hitting Enter or Return, or by choosing the page from the drop-down menu in the lower-left corner of the Document window.

Contextual menus

Contextual menus are menus that appear when you right-click (Windows) or control-click (Mac) the mouse. Contextual menus vary based on the element you click and the tool you are using. If no items are chosen, the contextual menu for the whole InDesign document appears, enabling you to pick features like zoom, paste, rulers, and guides. If an element is selected, you have the option of transforming, modifying, and editing it.

Contextual menus are sensitive to their surroundings (hence the name!). Remember to select a page element before right-clicking (Windows) or control-clicking (Mac) to get the contextual menu. If the object is not selected initially, the menu shown is for the document rather than the object.

Establishing the Workspace

Workspace settings are essential since they allow you to easily establish the desired layout. The global document settings govern components such as grids and guides that help align page elements. Guides and grids do not print when you print or publish a document.

Displaying and concealing grids and guidelines

Grids and guides are on-screen lines that assist in layout but which, by default, are not printed. A document grid is applied to the whole page area of the document. Use the document grid if you need to split a document into pieces to get the desired layout. Objects on a page may be aligned to the document grid, allowing for precise alignment and spacing of elements.

The baseline grid is another sort of grid that spans horizontally across the page. Employ the baseline grid to align text in various columns, resulting in a better website layout.

The document grid is used to align components on the page, whereas the baseline grid is used to align text across many columns.

❖ Select ViewGrids and Guides.show (or hide) the document grid to display or conceal the document grid.

❖ Select ViewGrids and Guides. Baseline Grid (Show/Hide) to show or hide the baseline grid.

There is an obvious distinction between these two types of grids. Guides are used to precisely position elements inside a layout and may be inserted anywhere on the page (or pasteboard). In contrast to grids, guides are usually developed separately. Use them to align certain items throughout a page, such as the tops of many photos. Items can snap to guidelines just like they can to a grid.

Follow these steps to build a guide and display or conceal it.

1. Ensure that the rulers are visible by selecting "Show Rulers."

   There are rulers at the workstation. If rulers are already displayed, the option "View Hide Rulers" is available from the View menu. Do not conceal the rulers.

2. Move the cursor to either a horizontal or vertical ruler.

   Ensure that the cursor is resting on a ruler.

3. Click the ruler and then drag the mouse to the page.

On the page, a ruler guide appears as a line.

4. Release the mouse button where you desire the guide to appear.

   You just made a ruler guide!

5. Select ViewGrids & HideGuides to hide the guide.

   This step conceals the newly-created guide but does not delete it. It is simple to reappear the guide in the following step.

6. Select ViewGrids and Guides Show Guides to display the guide again.

The created guide is displayed again on the page.

You can change the color of a ruler guide by positioning the mouse over it, clicking once to select it, and then right-clicking (Windows) or control-clicking (Mac) it and selecting a new color from the Ruler Guides menu.

In your preferences, you can also adjust the color of the guides and grid. To access them, select Edit Preferences Grids (Windows) or InDesign Preferences Grids (Mac OS X).When the Preferences dialogue box appears, you can change the color and spacing of the lines. To adjust the color settings for guides, click Guides & Pasteboards in the list on the left.

Alignment using a grid or a guide

You may align the page's components according to a grid or guide. Because they are precisely aligned to a grid or guide, grid or guide snapping is useful for aligning multiple elements without having to rely on your eyes. Select ViewGrids and Guides. Snap to ViewGrids & Guides or Document GridsSnap to Guides to ensure this setting is enabled. Clicking on these options will deselect them if they are already selected.

Using Smart Guides

Using InDesign's Smart Guides, you can align objects on a page with greater ease. Users of Illustrator and Photoshop may already be familiar with these interactive guides, but if you aren't, continue reading to learn how to utilize them.

Create two objects within an InDesign document to experiment with this feature. Any form or object will suffice!

Using the Selection tool, click and drag one object around another in a circular motion. As shown in Figure 1-8, guides will appear and disappear when objects are aligned with the top, center, or bottom of another object.

As illustrated in Figure 1-9, pink guidelines display by default when an item is aligned with the center of the page.

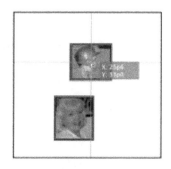

To view a print preview of your document, click the Preview Mode button located at the bottom of the Tools panel. Clicking this button removes all object bounding boxes, guides, and the grid.

Customized menus

InDesign has numerous menus with a variety of submenu options. It is probable that only a few of these menu options will be required. You can customize InDesign to hide menu items you don't use if you find yourself wading through a large number of menu items to locate the items you need.

Follow these instructions to customize your InDesign menus:

1. Select EditMenus to open the menu editor.
   The window for customizing menus appears.

2. In the Application Menu Command column, click the triangle beside the menu(s) you wish to modify.
   If you never anticipate importing XML, which is located

under the File menu, click the triangle to the left of the File menu to display this menu item.

3. Click the eye next to the menu item you wish to conceal.

Or, if you wish to highlight a menu item, you can add a color by clicking the color column to the right of the eye icon.

4. Click the Save As button at the top of the window to save the customized menu. Enter a name for your customized menu

set, click OK to save it, and then click OK a second time to close the Menu Customization window. The custom menus are preserved. To return to the original default menus or to further customize the menus, choose EditMenus whenever you are using InDesign.

Personalizing the look of the interface

In InDesign, you're able to modify the workspace's color scheme to alter its overall appearance. You can precisely adjust the darkness and brightness of the panels and pasteboard, or choose from a variety of preset options.

Follow these steps to customize the look of the InDesign interface:

1. Navigate to EditPreferencesInterface (Windows) or InDesign Preferences Interface (Mac). The Interface category is highlighted in the Preferences window upon launch. In the Appearance section at the top of this window, you can adjust settings that affect the UI's visual appearance.

2. Adjust the user interface and pasteboard's color scheme in the Appearance section. You can toggle between each setting, and InDesign will preview your selection, with Medium Dark as the default setting. Alternately, you can enter a custom percentage to adjust the brightness setting.

3. Select or clear the "Match Pasteboard

to Theme Color" checkbox.

By default, the option is selected, which darkens the pasteboard (the area surrounding your document). If you prefer a white poster, deselect this option.

4. Click the OK button to save your changes.

The look of the workspace is updated.

Storing a customized work area

You have seen that InDesign has a variety of panels. InDesign can remember the grouping of panels you use most often, including which ones are visible and which are hidden, if you notice that you use some panels more frequently than others. This is a workspace in InDesign. You may return to a previously saved workspace the next time you want a certain collection of panels to be open together. Workspaces are not tied to a specific document, so you can have one workspace for editing text and another for working on a layout.

Follow these steps to save a customized workspace.

1. Set up your InDesign

workspace the way you want to save it, with any panels you might need open at the same time.

The currently visible panels will be stored as a custom workspace.

2. From the menu, select Window Workspace, New Workspace.

The New Workspace dialog box is shown.

3. Select whether or not to save the panel menu locations and any customized menus. Enter a new name for the workspace in the Name text box.

Type in a name that tells what kind of work is done in this workspace, like "text editing" or "layout."

4. Click OK.

The personalized workspace is saved. On the Workspaces menu, the name you entered for your workspace is displayed.

Choose WindowWorkspace Your Workspace to access your workspace (where Your Workspace is the name you gave the workspace in Step 3).

If you no longer require the workspace to be saved, you can delete it. Simply choose Window WorkspaceDelete Workspace from the context menu.

Utilizing Documents

After becoming familiar with the InDesign workspace, you are prepared to begin working on a new document. After beginning to work on a document, you should learn how to import content from other programs and save it to your hard drive. When making layouts with InDesign, most of the content comes from other programs. These programs include Creative Cloud apps like Photoshop and Illustrator as well as non-Creative Cloud apps like Microsoft Word and Excel. You organize, modify, and incorporate text and images into a layout using InDesign. We begin by demonstrating how to import content and save new files.

Earlier in this chapter, in "Creating a New Publication" and "Opening an Existing Publication," you were shown how to open new and existing documents, respectively.

You might also be using a template. A template is a layout that you can use again and again by putting it on a document that needs a certain predesigned format. A company may use a template for its official letterhead, as each new letter requires the same page layout and design. Templates for InDesign use the ".indt" file extension.

Importing fresh material

Since you can import many different file types into an InDesign document, you can use many different types of content. Importing text, formatted tables, and images facilitates the creation of an effective layout. This capability facilitates integration with numerous programs.

Follow these steps to bring an image file into InDesign. In this case, we bring in a bitmap graphic file.

1. Select File > New > Document.
   The dialog box titled "New Document" appears.

2. Review the settings, make any necessary adjustments based on the size and type of document you wish to create, and then click the OK button.
   Opens a new document. Before

clicking OK, feel free to modify the settings to change the number of pages, page size, and intent.

3. Choose FilePlace.

The Place dialog box appears, allowing you to search for supported files on your hard drive. If you select the Show Import Options checkbox, another dialog box will appear prior to the import of the file.

Deactivate this option for the time being.

4. Select the file you wish to import, then click the Open button.

Certain file types, including bitmap photos, graphics, and PDFs, display a thumbnail preview at the bottom or to the right of the dialog box.

When you click the Open button, the Place dialogue box closes, and the cursor changes to an inverted L.

5. Click the area on the page where the upper-left corner of The imported file is placed on the page.

Click and drag to place the file into a specific frame

size, or if you've created an empty frame on the page, clicking on top of the frame places the text or image being imported within the frame.

A Ctrl-click (Windows) or -click (Mac) can be used to select multiple files. After selecting the images and clicking OK, each click places an image on the page. Alternatively, you can hold Shift+Ctrl (Windows) or Shift+ (Mac) while dragging a rectangle to have all selected images evenly spaced in a grid.

Note that when placing multiple images, you can view a thumbnail of each image prior to placing it.

You may also use the arrow keys on your keyboard to scroll through the loaded images.

Observing material

On the pages of your document, you can view elements in a variety of ways. For example, you may need to see objects on a page up close in order to make precise edits. InDesign provides multiple methods for document navigation:

❖ Scroll bars: The scroll bars allow you to navigate between pages. Below and to the right of the pasteboard, you will find the scroll bars. Click a scroll bar's handle and drag it to the left, right, or up.

❖ Zoom: Zoom into or out of the document to enlarge or reduce the document's display. To zoom in, select the Zoom tool (an icon of a magnifying glass) from the Tools panel and click anywhere on the page.

To zoom out, press Alt (Windows) or Option (Mac) and then click.

❖ Hand tool: Utilize the hand tool to navigate the page.

This tool is the fastest and most efficient method to browse documents and rearrange pages. While using a tool other than the Type tool, hit the spacebar to choose the Hand tool, then click and drag to navigate around the pasteboard.

❖ Keyboard: To zoom in using the keyboard, use Ctrl++ (Windows) or ++ (Mac); to zoom out, replace the plus sign with a minus sign.

Conserving your book

You do not want to lose your hard work needlessly, since even the most reliable systems and software might malfunction. It is essential to save a publication often so that you do not lose work if your computer or program breaks or the power goes out.

Choose FileSave or press Ctrl+S (Windows) or +S to save a file (Mac).

Also, you may choose to preserve several copies of your work. You may choose to do this if, for instance, you are experimenting with various design choices and wish to keep older versions of your files. To do this, utilize the Save As command, which makes it simple to create several copies of a document.

Select FileSave before continuing if you want the current document to retain any changes made since the last time it was saved. The updated version of the file contains all fresh updates to the document.

Follow these procedures to save a new version of the current document and then continue working on the new document:

1. Choose "File Save As."

   The Save As dialog box is shown.

2. Choose the location where you want to store the file.

3. Enter a new name for the document in the File Name area.

   This action saves a new file version. Consider a naming convention at this time. If your file is named myLayout.indd, you may rename it myLayout o2.indd to indicate the second version. The number may then be increased for each subsequent file version.

4. After you are done, click the Save button.

   This step saves the document with a new name in the specified directory.

The FileSave As command is also used for other purposes. You could consider saving your design as a template. After creating the template, choose FileSave As and then InDesign CC Template from the Save As type (Windows) or format (Mac) drop-down menu.

You can also select FileSave a Copy. This command saves a copy of the present state of the document under a new name, but you continue to work on the original document. These instructions are helpful for preserving incremental versions of a working project.

Working with Text and Text Frames

Text comprises the majority of the documents you generate; therefore, it is essential that you understand how to format, style, and manipulate text in your layouts. Text is composed of characters, which are stylized using certain typefaces.

You begin by editing and altering text put inside text frames—containers that carry text information on the page. The most significant things you can take away from this chapter are how to add text to documents and then modify the content to get the desired page layout.

Knowledge of Text, Fonts, and Frames

Text is often an important part of a publication because it tells the audience what the publication is about. It is essential to comprehend the terminology used in the following sections. The text and typeface are distinct from one another.

- ❖ Text is the letters, words, phrases, and paragraphs that make up the content of your publication's text frames.
- ❖ Font: the specific design of a group of characters that is used to style text. There are hundreds of font types available from several vendors, and many of them are bundled with the apps you install on your computer. InDesign's Font menu allows you to examine font faces and even set preferred fonts.

Similar to containers, frames are used to hold material. Two types of frames may be used in a publication:

- ❖ Text: The text that appears on your InDesign project's page. You can connect text frames so that text flows from one to the next, and you can wrap text around visual frames.
- ❖ Graphic: Displays an image placed inside a publication.

When you build frames in InDesign, they may include either text or images; thus, the processes for producing both kinds of frames are similar. InDesign makes frames fit the content automatically, so you can use both the frame and shape tools to build your layout and make frames with text or images in them.

Developing and Using Text Frames

Text frames hold any added text in a publication. You may generate a new text frame in a variety of ways. Text may be added to creatively drawn objects in InDesign, transforming them into text frames. Developing and using text frames in a publication is crucial due to the prevalence of text. Using three distinct tools, we demonstrate how to generate text frames in three distinct but significant ways in the following subsections.

Text frame creation using the Type tool

You may construct a text frame using the Type tool. If you use the Type tool and click the page without first creating a frame to contain the content, nothing occurs. Create a text frame with the Type tool as shown:

1. **T** Choose the Type tool from the Tools menu and position it on the page.

The cursor for the type tool is an I-bar. Position the cursor where you want to position the upper-left corner of the text frame.

2. Drag in a diagonal direction to form a text frame.

The mouse has a crosslike look when clicked. As demonstrated in Figure 2-1, as you drag, an outline of the text frame

emerges, indicating its proportions.

3. Release the mouse button when the frame's dimensions are right.

A text frame is generated, and an insertion point is set in the frame's upper-left corner. You may begin typing on the keyboard to input or import text. (Read the part under "Importing text.")

Using the Frame tool to format text

You may use the Frame tool to build rectangular, oval, and polygonal frames. After placing the frame on the website, you may convert it to a text frame, a graphic frame, or a simple design element. Follow these steps to build a new text frame using the Frame tool:

1. Using the Frame tool from the Tools menu, build a new frame by dragging diagonally.

The creation of a new frame on the page

2. Choose the type tool, then click inside the frame.

The X across the frame vanishes, and the frame becomes a text frame rather than a visual frame.

3. Choose the selection tool and move the text frame with it.

You can move the text frame by selecting it with the Selection tool and dragging it to a new location.

Form-based text frame creation

You can quickly turn an interesting form made with the drawing tools or copied and pasted from Illustrator into a text frame that can be filled with text. Just follow the instructions below:

1. Create a form with a stroke color and no fill using the Pen tool, Pencil tool, or Shape tool. Alternatively, copy and paste Illustrator artwork. On the page, a shape is produced that does not have a solid fill color.

2. Choose the Type tool from the menu of tools.
   The type tool is activated.

3. Enter text or import text by clicking inside the shape you established in Step 1.
   At this phase, the form is converted into a text frame. When you write, see how the text is contained inside the form.

Including Text in a Publication

In the step lists of the previous sections, you learned how to add text by clicking in the text frame and adding new material. Nevertheless, there are alternative methods to add text to publications. This is especially beneficial when using other programs to generate and update text-based documents.

The process of importing text

You may import text written or changed in other applications, including Adobe InCopy, Microsoft Word, and Excel. Because specialized text-editing software is frequently used prior to layout to revise manuscripts, importing changed text is a common process activity while preparing a publication. To import text into InDesign, proceed as follows:

1. Choose a file location.
   The Location dialog box appears. By exploring your hard drive, you may choose an importable file (such as a Word document, an InCopy narrative, or a plain text file).
2. Choose a file to import, and then click the Open button.
   The icon for inserting text, the

cursor, and a preview of the text appear. Drag the mouse to the location on the page where you want the upper-left corner of the text frame to appear after importing the document.

3. Click to position the imported text. This step imports the text and generates a text frame.

If you pick a text frame before importing text, the text is automatically positioned inside the text frame; hence, you would not need to use the cursor to position the text. After adding text, you may move the text frame wherever on the page and resize it if required.

Regulating text flow

Manage the text flow by using the following basic modifier keys while entering text:

❖ Choose FilePlace, then pick the file to import and click Open. Click the document when the loaded cursor transforms into a curved arrow while holding down the Shift key. The text is imported and flows automatically from one column to the next, or from one page to the next, until it runs out. InDesign can even generate pages if necessary.

❖ Choose FilePlace, then pick the file to import and click Open.

Maintain pressure on the Alt (Windows) or Option (Mac) key. Then, click and drag within a text box. (Don't let go of the Alt or Option keys!) When you continue to click and drag new text frames, the text flows from one text frame to the next until there is no more copy.

If the Display Import Options checkbox is selected in the Put window, a second window emerges from which you may remove styles and formatting from text and tables. This action brings in text that has not been formatted for editing.

Inserting filler text

Suppose you are creating a publication, but the text you need to import into it is not yet ready to be imported into InDesign; for example, the text is still being created or edited. Instead of waiting for the final text, you can continue to layout your publication using placeholder text.

Often, placeholder text is used to temporarily fill up a document. The text resembles conventional blocks of text, which is more natural than continually pasting the same few words into a text frame. Yet, placeholder text is not written in a specific language since it is only filler.

InDesign can automatically insert placeholder text into a text frame. This is how:

1. Build a text frame by picking the Type tool and dragging it diagonally across the page.

2. Select Type > Fill with Placeholder Text.

   Similar to the example in Figure 2-2, the text frame is automatically populated with letters and words.

Explore Africa Photo Safari

Pasting and copying text

You may copy and paste content from another program right into

InDesign to include it in a publication. If you choose to copy text in another application, you may instantly paste it into InDesign from the Clipboard. This is how:

1. Copy the text you wish to include in your document by pressing Ctrl+C (Windows) or +C (Mac).

   When you copy text, it is put on the clipboard (until it is changed), and you may paste it into InDesign.

2. Launch InDesign and press Ctrl+V (Windows) or +V (Mac) to paste the content into a new text frame.

   A new text frame emerges in the middle of the page, containing the chosen text.

You may also click within an existing text frame and hit Ctrl+V (Windows) or +V (Mac) to paste text from the clipboard straight into the frame. The same may be done with a picture.

Double-clicking a text frame allows you to access or change text, as well as enter or paste it into the frame. You may alter the formatting that is pasted into your document by modifying InDesign settings.

Choose all information (swatches, styles, etc.) or text only by selecting EditPreferences Clipboard Handling (Windows) or InDesignPreferences Clipboard Handling (Mac).

Examining the Text Frame Option

In the preceding parts of this chapter, you learned how to construct text frames and add text to them. In the sections that follow, we demonstrate how to order text frames in your publication to obtain the desired outcomes. Managing text frames so that they behave as desired requires knowledge of how they function once text has been inserted.

InDesign gives you complete control over the content of your publications. Adjusting the text frame settings enables you to modify the placement of text inside a frame. Updating these parameters is occasionally necessary when dealing with certain types of typefaces.

The context-sensitive menu for text frames includes several options for manipulating text frames. This menu allows you to conduct fundamental operations such as copying and pasting, filling the text frame with placeholder text, performing transformations, adding or modifying strokes, and changing the frame type. Retrieve the text frame by right-clicking (Windows) or control-clicking (Mac) a text frame, a contextual menu is shown. The majority of these features are also accessible through the Type and Object menus.

Adjusting choices for the text frame

Follow these steps to modify the text frame parameters that govern the appearance of text inside the frame:

1. Build a rectangle text frame on the page, then click it and choose ObjectText Frame Settings.

   To enter the Text Frame Options dialog box, you may alternatively use Ctrl+B (Windows) or +B (Mac) or utilize the contextual menu of the text frame.

   A chosen text frame is indicated by the presence of handles around its enclosing box.

The Text Frame Settings dialog box displays, displaying the chosen text frame's current settings.

2. Click the Preview checkbox to observe changes automatically.

   Now, any changes you make in the dialog box are immediately reflected on the page, allowing you to preview modifications before applying them.

3. In the Inset Spacing section of the dialog box, modify the Top, Bottom, and Left parameters, right and left values.

   These variables are used to offset text from the text frame's edges. The value you provide causes the text to be pushed inside the frame's edge. Only one of the four text fields requires a value when the Make All Settings Same switch is enabled.

   Text may also be indented, as explained in the section titled "Indenting Your Text" later in this chapter. You may select the vertical text alignment in this dialog box (top, center, bottom, or justify). You can align the text to the top or bottom of the text frame, center it in the frame vertically, or equally space the lines in the frame from top to bottom (justify).

4. Click OK when you are through making changes to this dialog box.

The modifications you made are implemented in the text frame.

Using and altering columns

When you create a new publication, you have the option to choose the number of columns it will include. Utilizing columns enables you to correctly align new text frames on the page by snapping them to columns. Even the gutter, which is the space between columns, may be adjusted.

Using the Text Frame Settings dialog box, you may also generate columns inside a single text frame. You may include up to 40 columns in a single text frame. When you add columns to a frame that already contains text, the content is automatically distributed across the columns. When designing a text-based layout in InDesign, you have three column options to pick from:

❖ When you have a specific number of columns in mind for a text frame, use Fixed Number.

❖ Employ Fixed Width when you are aware of the precise column widths that will appear in a text frame. As the text frame grows or shrinks, the number of columns may increase or decrease accordingly.

❖ Use Flexible Width if you want the column width to change based on the size of the text frame. Using Flexible Width, InDesign increases or decreases the number of columns based on the text frame's width.

The instructions below demonstrate how to add columns to a page's text frame:

1. Build a rectangle-shaped text box on the page.

Use the Text or Frame instrument to build the text frame. Text frames that are rectangular, oval, or even freehand forms created on the page might include columns.

2. After you create a text frame, the cursor will be placed inside the frame, and you can start typing text.

You can type in text by hand, copy and paste text from another document, or use TypeFill with Placeholder Text to add placeholder text.

3. Select the text frame and navigate to Object Text Frame Options.

You might want to check the Preview box in the Text Frame Options dialog box that opens so you can see right away how the changes you made to the settings affect the frame on the page.

4. Change the value in the Number text field within the Columns section.

In this example, the Number text field contains the value 2. The text within the selected text frame is divided into two columns. When you click on a different text field in the dialog box with Preview selected, the text frame on the page is updated to reflect the new value setting.

5. Modify the column width by entering a new value in the Width text box.

The column width is automatically determined based on the width of the text frame you created. In this example, we entered 10 (pixels) in the Width text

field. The size of the text frame depends on the width you specify for this column.

6. Change the value in the field labeled "Gutter."

The gutter value determines the distance between columns. If the gutter is too wide, enter a smaller number in the Gutter text field. For this example, we entered 0p5 in the Gutter text field to change the gutter width to half a point.

7. After you are finished, click OK

to make the changes.

The modifications are applied to the text frame you changed.

When you build columns in a text frame, you may adjust the frame by using the handles on its bounding box, as discussed in the subsequent section "Resizing and moving the text frame." The columns resize as required to split the text frame into the number of columns you chose in the Text Frame Options dialog box. If you choose the Fixed Column Width check box in the Text Frame Settings dialog box, your text frames are always the width you specify, no matter how you resize the text frame. When you adjust the text frame, the frame clamps to the selected fixed width.

You may also adjust the number of columns in the Control panel after choosing the text frame with the Selection tool or by using the paragraph options in the Control panel while using the Type tool.

Changing and Linking Text Frames on a Page

Making updates to text frames and then linking them to other text frames in a publication so that the tale may continue on a new page is crucial in most publications. You often deal with storylines of numerous paragraphs that need to continue on multiple pages in the text.

When you have a text frame on the page, you need to be able to change the size, position, and linking of the frame. You need to connect the frame to other frames on the page so that the text may flow between them, which is vital if you're constructing a layout that has a lot of text.

If you insert more text content than is visible in the text frame, the text still persists beyond the confines of the text frame; thus, if you have a text frame that's 20 lines tall but you paste in 50 lines of text, the final 30 lines are chopped off. You need to enlarge the text frame or have the text flow to another frame in order to view the remainder of the text you pasted. A little plus symbol (+) in a specific handle inside the text frame's enclosing box indicates that the frame contains additional material.

Adjusting the size and position of the text frame

While designing layouts, you often resize and move

text frames throughout the document as you determine how the page layout will appear. To resize and relocate a text frame, follow these steps:

1. Using the Selection tool, select a text frame on the page. There is a bounding box with handles on the page. A little red box with a red plus sign appears in the lower-right corner of the bounding box if the text frame has more text than it can display at the current size.

2. To resize the text frame, drag one of its handles.

As illustrated in Figures 2–3, the frame immediately refreshes on the website as you move the handles. Adjust the width or height by dragging the handles in the middle of each side of the frame, or simultaneously modify the height and width by dragging a corner handle. Shift-drag a corner handle to proportionately scale the text frame.

3. After resizing the text frame, click and drag it around the page by clicking in the center of a chosen frame.

You can move the frame around the page by clicking once within it and dragging it. A frame outline follows the pointer and indicates where the frame will be positioned when the mouse button is released. Release the frame after you are finished moving it.

If you use guidelines or grids on the page, the text frame will automatically align with them.

In addition, if you started a document with columns, the text frame will snap to the columns when you move it near the column guidelines.

You may also adjust the placement and size of a text frame using the Transform panel. If the Transform panel is not already visible, choose Window > Object and Layout > Transform. Then, follow the instructions below:

1. Modify the X and Y text boxes' values.

    To relocate the text frame to the upper-left corner of the page, enter 1 in both the X and Y text boxes.

    The text frame's X and Y coordinates (location) are updated to 1, 1. The little square in the center or along the edge of the text is the text frame's reference point. The X and Y coordinates you specified

correspond to this point's location.

Click any point on the reference point indicator in the upper-left area of the control panel to alter the reference point.

2. Modify the W and H values in the text areas.

    In this example, the W and H text boxes have the value 35 (picas). The width and height of the text frame adjust according to the specifications you select.

    Changing the frame's width and height using the

Transform panel is great if you need to define precise dimensions.

In addition to resizing and moving text frames, you may also alter their forms. Choose Direct Selection from the Tools panel after selecting a text frame. Afterwards, you may pick the text frame's corners and drag them to alter the text frame.

Combining text frames

If you wish to create page layouts with a great deal of text, you must understand how to string text frames together. Threading is the arrangement of text frames such that the text in one frame continues in the next.

Threading is important for the majority of layouts since it is not always possible to contain all text in a single frame. First, familiarize yourself with some of the relevant terminology, since Adobe has assigned unique names to connected text frames. Figure 22-4 depicts some of the ideas and symbols mentioned in the subsequent list.

An out port with text flowing
into another frame

When space runs
out for text in the
frame on the left
side, it has been
linked so that text
then runs into
the frame located

below it and to
the right. This was
done by linking
the text frames
together by clicking
on the out port on
one frame and then

An in port with text flowing from
another frame and an overset text indicator

- ❖ Flowing writing is defined as writing that starts in one frame and continues in another.

- ❖ Threading: Describes two text frames in which text flows from one frame to the next.

- ❖ The term given to a collection of phrases and paragraphs in

threaded text frames

- ❖ In port: A symbol on the upper-left side of a text frame's bounding box indicating that it is the first frame of a story or that text is flowing in from another frame.If an in-port icon features a little arrow, a narrative is flowing into it; otherwise, the in-port symbol is empty.

- ❖ Out port: An icon on the lower-right side of the text frame's bounding box that indicates text is flowing out of the frame. If the frame is linked to another text frame, the out port icon will feature a little arrow; otherwise, the out port symbol will be empty.

If a text frame is not linked to another frame and it contains overset text (more text than can be shown in a text frame), the Out port will display a little red plus sign (+).

Follow these steps to thread a block of text. For the best results, use a text block that contains whole phrases as opposed to placeholder text.

1. Copy some text to the Clipboard, for example, from the InDesign help files, a web page loaded in a web browser window, or a Word, Notepad, or SimpleText document.

The sort of text being pasted is irrelevant. You simply need to ensure that the text has at least a few paragraphs so that it can flow between frames.

In Figure 22-4, the text thread is

represented by a line linking successive text frames. By selecting View Extras—Show Text Threads, InDesign displays text threads.

2. Use the Type tool to generate two text frames on a single page.

Similar to the structure seen in Figure 2-5, the text frames might appear above or alongside one another.

This text is waiting for someplace to continue because it has run out of space in this small frame. It is just too much text for this

3. Using the Text tool, click the first text frame that is located above or to the left of the second text frame.

The flashing insertion point in the first text frame lets you know that you can type or copy and paste text into it.

4. Paste the text by pressing Ctrl+V (Windows) or +V

(Mac) into the text window.

Text transferred to the clipboard is pasted into the frame. If sufficient text has been pasted, the overset text icon (a red plus sign) appears in the lower-right corner of the text frame. (Please see Figure 2-5.) If the overset text symbol does not appear, use the Paste command a second time to add extra text to the frame.

5. Select the overlaid text symbol with the Selection tool.

The cursor transforms into a loaded text icon, allowing you to pick or create a new text frame to continue the story.

6. Click the second text frame while the cursor is over it. When the pointer hovers over the second text frame, it turns to the thread text icon. When the second text frame is selected, the two frames are threaded since the text continues in the second frame.

You may continue to create and thread frames. You may list them on the same page or on pages that follow.

Moreover, you may unthread text, which breaks the connection between two text frames. You may alter the frames used to thread text, for example, by changing the page on which the tale continues when it is threaded to a second text frame. To break the connection, double-click the In port or Out port symbol of the text frame you want to unthread. The frame is then unthreaded (but no text is removed).

Click LayoutPagesInsert Pages if your document does not have multiple pages. After entering the number of pages to be added, click the OK button. Using the Page Field control at the bottom of the workspace, you can now navigate among the pages and create a new text frame into which you may connect your content.

Adding a page jump number

You may add a page jump number (text that specifies where the tale continues if it jumps to a text frame on another page) to an existing file if your document contains several pages. Ensure a narrative thread exists between text frames on two separate pages before beginning, and then follow these steps:

1. Start a new text frame on the first page and continue typing on the second.

2. Select the newly created text frame with the Selection tool.

3. Move the text frame so it slightly overlaps the story text frame.

   InDesign should know which text frame it is following the story from or to.

As illustrated in Figure 2-6, overlap the two text frames (and maintain them overlapped) so that InDesign knows to correlate these text frames (the continued-notice text frame and the tale text frame) with one another.

Thereafter, you may group these two text frames so

that they move together.

Choose an object group while both text frames are highlighted. (Click while holding Shift to pick both text frames using the Selection tool.)

4. Double-click the new text frame containing the content continuing on the page to position the insertion point at the desired location for the page number. Be certain that a space follows the previous character since the page number is put at the insertion point.

5. Select Type From the Type menu, select Insert Special Character MarkersNext Page Number. Including a number into the text frame. The page number is sensitive to the position of the following threaded text frame; hence, if you change the second text frame, the page number will immediately update.

Repeat these steps if the story continues; in Step 5, select TypeInsert Special

CharacterMarkersPrevious Page Number instead.

Understanding Paragraph Settings

There are several methods to modify the parameters for a complete text frame or a single paragraph inside a text frame. You may use the Paragraph panel to modify the indentation, justification, and alignment of a single paragraph or an entire text frame. To display the Paragraph panel, choose WindowType and TablesParagraph.

If you want changes made in the Paragraph panel to apply to all text frames on the page, you must first select the whole text frame or frames on the page before making any changes.

Then, the choices you make in the Paragraph panel effect all paragraphs inside the chosen text frames, as opposed to just one. If you want the choices you make in the Paragraph panel to affect just one paragraph inside a text frame, you must first select that paragraph using the Type tool before making your changes.

Italicizing your text

With the Paragraph panel, you may indent a paragraph in a tale. The indentation distances the paragraph from the text frame's bounding box. How to alter the indentation:

1. Build a text frame and fill it with text on the page.
   Text may be entered manually, copied, and pasted, or placeholder text can be inserted by selecting TextFill with Placeholder Text.

2. Make sure the insertion point is flashing inside the text frame of the paragraph you want to edit, or select the text frame with the Selection tool.

3. Choose WindowType and TablesParagraph to bring up the paragraph panel.
   The Paragraph panel opens, displaying the current text frame settings.
   Figure 2-7 displays the names of each configuration control.

4. Modify the value in the Left Indent text box and hit the Enter key.
   The indentation increases in size as the number increases. When you type text, you may define the unit

of measurement by typing "in" for inches or "pt" for points, using any forms of measurement that InDesign allows.

5. Adjust the first line's left indent value and hit Enter.

To modify all paragraphs in a narrative, click the insertion point inside a paragraph and choose Edit/Select All before modifying the parameters.

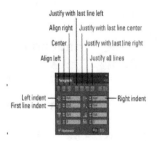

Alignment and justification of text

Text frames may be formatted using the Alignment and Justification buttons in the Paragraph panel:

❖ Align allows you to align text to the left, center, or right corners of text frames.

❖ Justification enables you to align text with the boundaries of the text frame and to justify the last line of text in a paragraph.

Click the Align or Justify button to align or justify a

block of text, respectively. Figure 2-7 displays the Align and Justify controls found in the Paragraph panel.

Keeping a paragraph format

Get the perfect indentation, font, and spacing for your content, only to realize that you must apply these properties a hundred times to finish your project? Conversely, have you ever determined that the indentation is excessive? Wouldn't it be convenient to modify one indentation text field and have it affect all other instances? With InDesign, you can do this using paragraph styles.

Use these steps to design a paragraph format:

1. Build a text frame, add text, and apply a customizable first-line indent. Pick some text; you do not need to choose all of it.

2. Choose Window Styles and Paragraph Styles from the menu. Opens the Paragraph Styles panel.

3. Choose a new paragraph style from the menu in the Paragraph Styles window.

The dialog box for New Paragraph Style opens. Notice that in this unidentified style, every characteristic— font, size, and indentation—has already been recorded. At this stage, you just need to provide the style.

4. Replace Paragraph Style 1 with a more relevant name, such as "BodyCopy," and click OK.

Your style is crafted! The dialog box closes when you click OK, and the new style is added to the Paragraph Styles panel list. Double-clicking on the style's name in the Paragraph Styles panel will allow you to alter its parameters.

By choosing the frame and clicking the style in the Paragraph Styles panel, you may apply the style to other text frames.

If you want to change an existing style, you can do so on the left side of the New Paragraph Style dialogue box.Choose an item from the list to look at and change the paragraph attributes for that item on the right side of the dialog box. This will change all places where the selected paragraph style is used.

When you need to use a certain set of styles for a template, you can import those styles from other documents or a file on your hard drive. Choose Load Paragraph Styles from the Paragraph Styles panel menu to import paragraph styles. A dialog box invites you to locate a file on your hard disk. Choose the file to load and press the OK button.

Editing Narratives

Your papers undoubtedly include several types of content, some of which may need editing. InDesign has a story editor for text editing. When it is awkward or impossible to launch another text editor, this capability might be handy.

InDesign is also compatible with another Adobe application, InCopy. It is a text editor comparable to Microsoft Word with InDesign integration features for efficient page layout. If you work in IT or editorial management and have users who just write and others who only handle layout, you should consider InCopy as a potential text editor.

Using the narrative editor

The InDesign story editor allows you to format text and examine a story outside of small columns. Follow these steps to access the story editor and modify a piece of text:

1. Find the text you want to change and select the text frame with the Selection tool. A box with handles emerges around the text frame.

2. In Story Editor, choose EditEdit or press Ctrl+Y (Windows) or +Y (Mac) on the keyboard to change the story. The story editor opens inside the InDesign workspace in a new window.

3. Make any required edits to the text in the window and then click the Close button. Your narrative displays as a single block of text. Whatever paragraph styles you apply to the text in the story editor are shown in the left-hand information pane.

Figure 2-8 demonstrates that tables may be seen in the narrative editor. In the narrative editor, the table may be collapsed and expanded by clicking the little table icon.

Table icon

Select TypeTrack Changes.Track Changes in the Current Story if you want to make text modifications while maintaining the original content. In the story editor, both the original and updated text remain, but in layout mode, only the edited content displays. Subsequently, you (or an editor) may use the Story Editor's Track Changes command to approve or reject text updates.

Checking for spelling errors

It is simple to commit grammatical and spelling mistakes. When printing or exporting a document to PDF, it is necessary to check for misspelled words.

This is how to do a spelling check in InDesign:

1. Select Edit > Spelling > Check

Spelling from the menu.

2. In the resulting Check Spelling dialog box, pick a search option from the Search drop-down list, and then click the Start button.
The spell checker begins scanning the text or file automatically.

3. Choose from three options:

- Use the Skip button to disregard an incorrectly spelled word.

- Choose a suggested spelling change from the list in the box labeled "Suggested Corrections" and click "Change."

- Click Ignore All to disregard all future occurrences of that term.

In the text frame, the misspelling is repaired before moving on to the next misspelling.

4. Click the Done button to end the spell check; alternatively, click OK when InDesign notifies you that the spell check is complete.

Even when using the spell-check function to edit your writing, it is always a good idea to carefully proofread your work. The spell checker will not detect grammatical faults or improper word use.

Using individualized spelling dictionaries

By selecting the Add button, you can simply add terms, such as proper nouns, to your dictionary.

You can make a user dictionary from scratch or import one from an older version of InDesign, a file sent to you by someone else, or a server. The vocabulary you add is used for all of your documents in InDesign.

Follow the instructions below to build your own personalized dictionary:

1. Choose Edit > Preferences > Dictionary (Windows) or InDesign > Preferences > Dictionary (Mac OS X) (Mac). The Dictionary section appears in the Preferences dialog box.

2. Select your dictionary's language from the Language drop-down menu.

3. Click the "New User Dictionary"

option under the Language menu.

4. Choose the user dictionary's name and location, and then click OK (Mac) or Save (Windows).

If you want to see when a spelling mistake occurs without opening the Check Spelling dialog box, select EditSpellingDynamic Spelling. Thereafter, unknown words are highlighted. Right-click (Windows) or -click (Mac) the word and select the appropriate option from the contextual menu, or add the word to your dictionary.

Using Tables

A table is composed of columns and rows, which separate its cells. Daily, you encounter tables on television, in print publications, and on the Internet. In actuality, a calendar is a table: each month's days are listed in a column, each week is a row, and each day is a cell. You may utilize tables for a variety of purposes, like listing items, personnel, and events.

The list below covers the table components and how to edit them in InDesign:

❖ Rows: Stretch across a table horizontally. You

may customize the row height.

- ❖ Columns: In a table, columns are vertical. You may alter a column's width.
- ❖ Cells: A text frame You may insert information into this frame and format it as you would any other InDesign text frame.

Developing tables

The simplest approach to making a table is to have the necessary data on hand. (Note that this is not the only option.) But the most dynamic approach to exploring what InDesign can do with tables is to import existing data.

Follow the steps below to explore table functionality:

1. Create a text area and input material formatted with tabs.

The sample includes event dates:

Summer Events

June	July	August
1	2	3
4	5	6

Observe that the text was simply entered by pressing Tab between each subsequent entry. The text is not even required to be aligned.

2. Choose the text and select Table > Convert Text to Table from the menu.

The Options dialogue window for Converting Text to Tables appears. There, you may choose columns or allow the tabs in your text to define the columns. Learn more about table styles in the section titled "Building table styles." You may assign a table style concurrently with text-to-table conversion.

3. To accept the default settings, click OK.

4. While holding the Shift key, click and drag the right boundary with the mouse to expand or contract the table.

The cells accommodate the increased table size appropriately.

5. Click and drag over the top three cells, then choose Table Merge Cells to combine them.

Follow these procedures to create a new table without the current text:

1. Make a new text box with the Type tool.

The insertion point should flash in the newly created text frame. Double-click the text frame to activate the insertion point (I-bar) if it is not flashing or if you built a new frame in another manner. You cannot build a table in a text frame unless the insertion point is active.

2. Select TableInsert Table.

3. In the Insert Table dialog box, enter the number of rows and columns you want to add to the table in the Rows and Columns text areas, and then click OK.

We generated a table with six rows and three columns, for instance.

Adjusting table settings

You can handle several table arrangements. Change the text, fill, and stroke characteristics of individual table cells or the whole table in InDesign. Due to its adaptability, you may design totally customized tables to show data in a unique and intuitive manner. In this part, we cover the most fundamental table editing choices.

To begin modifying table settings, go as follows:

1. Choose the table you want to modify by clicking inside a cell.

2. Choose Table > Table Options > Table Setup.
   The Table Setup tab is selected when the Table Options dialog box appears.
   The dialog box offers multiple tabs with options that may be modified for various table components.
   Under the Table Setup tab, you may modify the table's columns, rows, border, and spacing, as well as specify how column or row strokes are shown in relation to one another. For instance, we changed the number of rows and columns and the border weight of the table to a 3-point stroke.

3. Choose the "Preview" option at the bottom of the dialogue box.
   You may examine the changes you make to the page while using the

dialog box by using Preview.

4. Select the Row Strokes tab and modify the available parameters.

For this example, we chose Every Second Row from the Alternating Pattern drop-down menu, modified the Table Border Weight to 2, and set the Color property for the first row to C = 15, M = 100, Y = 100, K = 0 (the CMYK equivalent of red).

This action results in every other row having a red, 2-point stroke. You may also click the Column Strokes tab to modify column stroke characteristics. The two tabs function identically.

5. Select the Fills tab and modify the available settings.

In this example, we chose Every Other Row from the Alternating Pattern drop-down menu, modified the Color property to the CMYK equivalent of red, and kept the Tint parameter at its default value of 20 percent. This step tints the first and alternate rows with a crimson hue.

6. Choose OK.

   The table is updated with the modifications made in the Table Options dialog box.

7. Click a table cell until the insertion point begins to flicker.

   The table cell has been chosen.

8. Locate a picture that can be copied to the clipboard, and then press Ctrl+C (Windows) or +C (Mac) to copy the image to the clipboard.

9. Return to InDesign and paste the picture into the table cell using Ctrl+V (Windows) or +V (Mac OS) (Mac).

   The height or width (or both) of the table cell adjusts depending on the proportions of the picture. Verify if the insertion point is active in the cell if the picture cannot be pasted.

You may modify not just the table itself but also the cells inside it. To enter the Cell Options dialog box, choose Table > Cell Options Text from the menu bar.

Moreover, you may modify each cell using the Paragraph panel. Similarly, the Tables panel allows you to modify the number of rows and columns as well as their widths and heights. To access the Tables panel, choose WindowType and TablesTable.

You may import tables from other applications, such as Excel, into InDesign. To import a spreadsheet, choose FilePlace from the menu bar. The spreadsheet is imported into InDesign as a table, which may then be edited as required.

Developing table formats

If you've spent time tweaking your table's strokes, fills, and spacing, you should definitely save it as a style. Designing a table style allows you to reuse your table arrangement for subsequent tables. Use these steps to produce a table format:

1. Create a table with the desired aesthetic. The simplest technique to design a table style is to finish the table configuration and make the table seem as desired.

2. Identify the table.

   To choose a text with the text tool, click and drag.

3. Choose Window Styles and Table Styles from the menu.

   The Panel for Table Styles displays

4. While pressing and holding the Alt (Windows) or Option (Mac) key, click the "Create New Style" button at the bottom of the Table Styles window.

   The dialog box titled "New Table Style" displays.

5. Give the style a name and click OK.

   Your table's characteristics are preserved as a style.

To modify the properties of a table style, just double-click the style's name in the Table Styles panel. (Ensure that no options are chosen.)

Examining Literature along a Path

Text on a route may be used to produce some fascinating effects. The Type on a Path tool allows you to curve text along a line or form. This function is very handy when you want to generate unique page title effects.

Follow these procedures to insert text on a path:

1. With the Pen tool, draw a path on the paper. Construct at least one curve on the route after its creation. (Read Chapter 4 of this minibook to learn how to confidently use the Pen tool.)
2. Choose the Type on a Path tool by clicking and holding down the Type tool.
3. Position the cursor close to the route you just constructed.

When the cursor is near a path, a plus sign (+) shows next to it, and you may click and begin typing on the route.

4. Click on the plus sign and enter some text on the route.

After clicking, an insertion point appears at the beginning of the route, and you may add text along the path. You choose the type on a route by dragging over the text to highlight it, as you would with any other text.

To change the attributes of a type on a path, open the Type on a Path Options dialog box by selecting TypeType on a PathOptions.With the Type on a Path Options dialog box, you may adjust the placement of each character on the path using effects. You may also reverse the text, modify the letter spacing, and change the character alignment to the path in the Align drop-down menu or to the path stroke in the To Path drop-down menu. Explore the parameters to see how they impact your type. To make changes, click OK; to reverse actions, use Ctrl+Z (Windows) or +Z (Mac OS X) (Mac).

To conceal the path while leaving the text visible, set the path's stroke weight to 0 pt.

Understanding Page Layout

This shows you how to put pictures and words together so you can start making page layouts. A magazine's pictures and words stand out more when the pages are laid out in interesting and creative ways. People are more likely to read what you post on a page if the layout is interesting.

Importing Images

Several types of picture files may be added to an InDesign document. Common formats include AI, PSD, PDF, JPG, PNG, and TIF. Importing images into graphic frames. You may design the frames before to importing, or if you don't have one, InDesign will make one for you when you add the picture to the page.

When you print or export the final product, you must use the original picture that you imported into your InDesign layout. You use special controls to keep an eye on the connected picture and change certain parameters, like the quality and color of the image. When you import a picture, you can also use the Image Import Options dialog box to access extra

parameters. In the section titled "Importing other InDesign documents" later in this chapter, you will learn how to modify different import settings.

For now, you can use these steps to add a picture to your InDesign layout:

❖ Ensure that nothing is chosen on the page.
   If an item is chosen on the page, click an empty area to deselect everything before continuing.
❖ Choose FilePlace.
   The Location dialog box will popup, allowing you to navigate your hard drive.

for picture file importation. This dialog window may be used to import numerous InDesign can import more than just photos.

❖ Choose the picture to import, then click Open.

The Put dialog box closes, and the pointer shows a thumbnail of the currently selected file picture you have chosen.

Several photos may be imported simultaneously into an InDesign layout. Simply when holding down Ctrl (Windows) or (Mac), pick several files in the Location dialogue box.

❖ Position the cursor where you would want the upper-left corner of the Click the mouse to position the first picture on the page.

If you have numerous photographs chosen, you may use the left and right arrow keys.

Using the arrow keys to browse the thumbnail photos in your loaded cursor clicking the page's link after a page click, the subsequent picture is put until no more photos may be placed.

Pictures are imported and put into a graphic element in the publication frame. The picture may be resized, moved, and modified with the modify the frame and picture using the selection or Direct selection tool by use the Selection tool.

When inserting several photographs, you may place all the chosen images in one step by hitting Shift+Ctrl (Windows) or Shift+ (Mac) while dragging a rectangle with the mouse.

This will equally position the images in a grid.

Don't be concerned if the imported picture is too big for the layout or must be trimmed.

It might be simpler to construct an empty graphic frame and then add an image.

Picture to it than to simultaneously import the image and generate the frame. Before importing a picture, you may construct an empty frame and adjust its fitting characteristics, so that the image fits appropriately when it is imported. To adjust the frame's fitting parameters, choose

ObjectFittingFrame Fitting Options.

Importing PDFs

PDF files may be imported and placed as images in InDesign layouts. You may preview and trim pages during importation using the Insert PDF dialog box. You import one page at a time, therefore you must utilize the Advance and Back buttons provided beneath the preview to pick a page to insert. Moreover, you cannot import video, sound, or buttons, and you cannot alter the PDF after it has been imported into InDesign; thus, it is similar to importing a JPG file.

The Put PDF dialog box has these options:

❖ Crop To: You may crop the imported page using this drop-down menu list. Certain alternatives may be inaccessible due to the contents of the inventory. The PDF being imported. The hatching outline in the preview reveals the following crop markings

❖ Translucent Background: Choosing this option makes the PDF transparent background translucent so that page components are visible through. If this option is selected, the PDF backdrop is imported as solid white is not chosen.

If your monitor is big enough to see your document window and computer directories, you may drag and drop picture files straight into your layout without using the Put command.

Importing documents created in InDesign

With InDesign, you may insert one document inside another. This function could that may seem unusual, yet it has numerous applications. For instance, if you want to advertise a page from a book in a catalog, you may import a picture of the page without first converting it to an image format. This method eliminates a step and generates a higher-quality version of the picture being inserted into InDesign.

Here's how to make use of this function:

1. With a document open, choose FilePlace or press Ctrl+D (Windows) or +D (Mac OS) on the keyboard (Mac).

   The Place dialogue box is shown.

2. Check the option to Display Import Options at the bottom of the Location menu dialog box.

3. Double-click a specific InDesign file to open it.

   As illustrated in Figure 3-1, the Put InDesign Document dialog box opens, allowing you to choose the page or pages you want to insert.

4. Click the Accept button.

5. Click the page to position the file.

   If you are putting together a multi-page document, click again to insert each additional page.

Linking and Embedding Images

Images that you import may either be linked to

your document or integrated into it. The distinction between linking and embedding is as follows:

- ❖ Linking: The picture shown in an InDesign document is a glimpse of an image saved somewhere on your computer or network. If the linked file is modified, your InDesign document must be updated.
- ❖ Embedding: The picture is copied into the InDesign document and preserved there. An embedded picture is copied and saved immediately inside the InDesign document, regardless of where the source file is stored or if the file has been modified.

When you print or export a document, InDesign utilizes the associated photos to generate the required information to produce a high-quality printed page, PDF file, or web-ready image. InDesign monitors connected files and notifies you if any are moved or modified. You may edit image links by selecting the picture in the Links panel and selecting

Update Link or Relink from the panel's menu. To connect the file to the new location, you must first locate it on your hard drive. Likewise, if you give someone your InDesign file, be sure to include all of its connected files.

If you embed photographs instead of linking to them, the file size of your publication will increase due to the additional data contained in them. Examine the Links panel to determine whether files are embedded or linked. Choose WindowLinks to access the panel and see if any linked or embedded pictures are shown.

You may embed a file by utilizing the options in the Links panel. If you wish to embed a linked file inside the document, click the triangle in the upper-right corner to enter the panel menu, then pick Embed Link.

Instead, choose Unembed Link from the Link panel's menu to link a file instead of embedding it in the document. We suggest connecting to all photos so that your files do not get too huge and so that you may alter the image files independently.

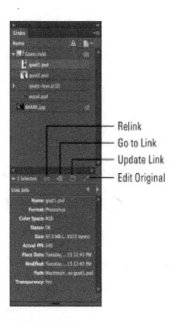

— Relink
— Go to Link
— Update Link
— Edit Original

Adjusting the display and image quality

When photos are included in an InDesign layout, you may choose the quality parameters that will affect how they are shown. If your computer is older or slower than usual, or if you have a lot of photographs, these adjustments could be able to speed up your work.

It may be possible to avoid having to print the project several times for proofing if photos are shown at a higher quality. This will give you a better idea of the completed print job. These options do not affect the final printed or exported result; rather, they simply affect how you see the photos while using InDesign to produce a page.

To change the picture display quality on a Mac, go to Edit > Preferences > Display Performance or InDesign > Preferences > Display Performance. Next, from the Default

View drop-down box, choose one of the options below:

- ❖ Fast: The whole picture or graphic is grayed out to improve performance.
- ❖ Typical (default): Bitmaps have a tendency to seem a little blocky when using this option, especially when zoomed in. If you choose this option, zooming in and out happens more quickly. The picture is shown on the screen by InDesign using a preview that it either developed or that was previously imported with the file.
- ❖ Good quality: The picture that appears onscreen is the original. Using this option may cause InDesign to run slowly, but you may see a precise representation of the final layout.

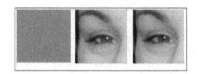

Choose the graphic frame and select ViewDisplay Performance to modify the display for a specific picture. Choose one of the

224

three choices from the submenu after that.

Choosing images

When importing a picture into a document, you may use the Selection or Direct Selection tools to choose that image in a variety of ways. Depending on whether you want to pick and change just the graphic frame or only the picture within it, it's important to apply the various approaches.

These procedures should be followed in order to pick and alter a picture on the page:

1. Import the picture into InDesign and place it on a page.

A graphic frame surrounds the picture.

2. Using the Selection tool, move one of the graphic frame's corner handles toward the frame's center.

The picture is not changed, just the graphic frame. While the picture retains the same size inside the frame, as seen in the middle of Figures 3-4, it seems to have been cropped since you changed the size of the graphic frame.

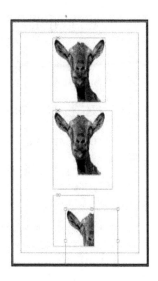

3. Choose Edit-Undo or press Ctrl+Z (Windows) or +Z (Mac) to undo picture modifications.

The picture is restored to its previous position on the page.

4. Continue using the Selection tool to click the image's center, where a circle appears, and drag the image into the frame.

The size of the frame stays the same, but its contents are shifted. You may also use the Selection tool to move the frame and its contents by clicking anywhere inside the frame; however, it is recommended that you click on the frame's center since this works for both the Selection and Direct Selection tools.

5. Choose the Direct Selection tool, then

click and drag inside the picture to reposition it within the graphic's frame-bounding box.

As you move the cursor over a graphic, a hand appears; when you move the picture slightly outside the graphic frame borders, that portion of the image is no longer visible; it does not print and is not exported.

By selecting ObjectFitting and one of the available options, you can resize a frame or picture.Even before placing an image, you may choose this aspect ratio, which is extremely useful for constructing templates. To resize a picture, select ObjectFittingFrame Fitting Options before placing it.

The Links panel may assist you in locating photos inside documents, opening images for editing, and displaying pertinent information about chosen images. Figure 3-2 may help you explore the

Links panel and properly manage your photographs.

Modifying Text and Images in a Layout

InDesign provides several options for combining text and visuals in a layout. From the tools in the Tools panel to commands and panel settings, InDesign provides extensive control over the modification of visuals and text inside a spread.

Page dimensions and orientation

While creating a new document, you may choose the direction and size of the pages. If you ever need to modify your document's settings after you've generated it, choose FileDocument Setup and modify the following choices, which affect all pages:

❖ Page Orientation: Choose between portrait and landscape mode. When you create a new document, page orientation is one of the first decisions you must make. Landscape pages are wider than they are tall, and portrait pages are taller than they are broad.

❖ Page Size: Select from a variety of

predefined standard page sizes, including letter, legal, and tabloid. You may also provide a custom page size for the document. Ensure that the page size corresponds to the kind of paper you will be printing on or the screen size if you are publishing your work online.

Also, you may utilize the pages panel to modify the size of individual pages and create pages of varying sizes.

Columns, margins, and gutters

The use of margins, columns, and gutters facilitates layout and limits the size of a page.

❖ The space between the page's edge and the primary printed area. The four margins (top, bottom, left, and right) form a rectangle around the edge of the page. When printing or exporting a publication, the margins do not print.

❖ Column: Separate a page into parts

used for text and image layout on a page. Beginning with a page that contains at least one column between the margins. Column guides, represented by a pair of lines separated by a gutter space, may be added. Column guidelines are not printed when the publication is exported or printed.

❖ The horizontal gap between two columns on a page A gutter prevents columns from overlapping. You may choose the width of the gutter by selecting ObjectText Frame Settings.

Nevertheless, you may also adjust the margins and columns of a document after it has been produced and give different values for each page. The gutter, which is the width of the gap between each column, is modifiable.

With the Margins and Columns dialog box, you may specify new settings for margins and columns. Select LayoutMargins and Columns, then edit each page separately.

Columns and margins are important for positioning and aligning page items. These guides allow you to precisely position several things on a page by allowing objects to snap to them.

Using guidelines and snapping

Utilizing guidelines while designing page layouts is a smart idea since they allow for more exact alignment and positioning of page components and layout items. Visually aligning items is challenging since it is frequently impossible to see if an object is slightly out of alignment until you zoom in significantly.

ViewGrids and Guides Snap to Guides can be enabled to enable snapping. Snapping makes guidelines and grids handy. As you pull an item near a grid, it becomes magnetically attracted to the line. After creating a guide, aligning an item to it is simple, and you'll see that InDesign shows temporary guides when you move an object close to another object or a guide.

Since guidelines are important while building a layout, consider the following InDesign-supported varieties:

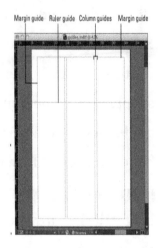

Margin guide   Ruler guide   Column guides   Margin guide

❖ Column guides are used to evenly divide a page into columns and align text frames in a document. These guidelines are established when you start a new document with several columns in InDesign.

After a document has been set up, you can also change the column guides by choosing LayoutMargins and Columns.

❖ Margin guides: Specify the space between the page's perimeter and the primary printing area. (These guidelines are discussed in the prior section.)

❖ Ruler guides are made by hand and can be used to line up images, measure objects, or indicate where a certain layout component should go.Go to Chapter 1 of this manual for information on how to add ruler guidelines to the workspace.

❖ Smart guides: As discussed earlier, smart guides allow you to align elements on an InDesign page with other objects or even with the page itself. Smart Object Alignment enables simple snapping to page item centers, page borders, and page centers. In addition to snapping, smart guides provide the user with feedback on the item being snapped to.

❖ Liquid guidelines: liquid guidelines are important when designing layouts for a range of tablet devices.

You may eliminate all guidelines simultaneously in InDesign CC by right-clicking the ruler (Windows) or control-clicking the ruler (Mac) and choosing Delete All Guides on Spread from the contextual menu.

Securing items and guides

You may put items such as objects and guidelines in place. This function is very handy when you have precisely positioned page components. Locking items or guides prevents them from being moved accidentally from their current location.

To lock an element, follow these steps:

1. Create a page item with a drawing tool, then select it with the Selection tool. When the item is chosen, a bounding box with handles displays.
2. Select ObjectLock. The item is secured in place. Now, when you attempt to move the item using the Selection or Direct Selection tools, it remains in its present place.

Follow these steps to secure guidelines:

1. Drag a few ruler guidelines onto the page by clicking inside a ruler and dragging in the direction of the page. There is a line on the page. If rulers are not visible around the pasteboard, select ViewRulers.
2. If necessary, drag a ruler guide to a new spot; when satisfied with the arrangement of the ruler guidelines,

choose ViewGrids and GuidesLock guides.

Every guide inside the workspace is locked. If you attempt picking up a guide and moving it, the guide stays in its existing place and cannot be changed.

If there are any column guides on the page, they are also locked. Employ layers to organize various sorts of material, including guides, in your publications. Layers are similar to transparencies that sit on top of one another; therefore, they may be used to stack page components. For instance, you may like to put related elements (such as photos or text) on the same layer. Each layer has its own bounding box color, allowing you to tell which objects are on which layer.

Combining text and images

Text and images on a website should flow together and go well with each other for a good layout. You may use text wrap to provide visual continuity between text and visuals. You will learn how to wrap text around photos and graphics in your publications in this part.

Enclosing objects in text

Text may be wrapped around images, as seen in Figures 3-6. Wrapping is a common element in print and web page layouts. You may choose several text wrapping choices using the Text Wrap panel, which you can access by selecting Window Text Wrap. Use the five buttons located at the top of the panel to set the text wrapping style for the selected item. Underneath the buttons are text fields where offset settings for the text wrap may be entered. If an option is not accessible, the fields will be grayed out.

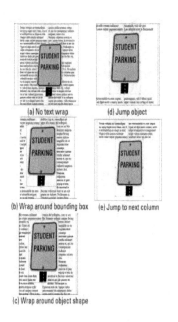

(a) No text wrap

(d) Jump object

(b) Wrap around bounding box

(e) Jump to next column

(c) Wrap around object shape

Using the drop-down menu at the bottom of the Text Wrap panel, you can choose one of many contour possibilities. The following list illustrates what occurs when you wrap text around an object's form using one of these buttons:

❖ No Text Wrapping: Uses the option by

default to eliminate text wrapping from the specified item.

❖ Wrap around Bounding Box: wraps text around all edges of the bounding box of the object.

❖ Wrap around Object Shape: Wraps text around the perimeter of an object.

❖ Jump Object: Causes the text wrapping around the picture to leap from above the image to below it, with no text wrapping to the left or right of the column object.

❖ Next Column: Place the end of the text over the image, then move to the next column. There is no wrapping of text to the left or right of the picture.

❖ Offset: Input offset values to wrap text around the whole item.

❖ Wrap Options: Choose an option to specify on which sides the text will wrap.

❖ Contour Options: Choose a contour from this drop-down menu to instruct InDesign on how to identify the image's edges.

To detect around an item or image, you can choose from a variety of vector pathways or transparent edges.

Follow these procedures to apply text wrapping to an item (a sketch or an image):

1. Construct a text frame on a website containing an image.

Append text to the text frame by entering, copying, or populating it with placeholder text. This text will wrap around the picture; thus, the text frame should be somewhat bigger than the graphic frame.

2. Pick a graphic frame on the page and slide it over the text frame using the Selection tool.

Box handles appear at the image's or graphic's perimeter.

3. Select WindowText Wrap to open the Text Wrap panel.

Opens the Text Wrap panel.

4. Click the "Wrap around Object Shape" button while the graphic frame is still chosen.

Instead of hiding behind the picture, the text is wrapped around it.

5. Select Detect Edges or Alpha Channel from the Contour Options drop-down menu if you are dealing with an image that has a transparent backdrop.

Customizing a text wrap

Once you have applied a text wrap to an object (like we showed in the previous section), you may alter that text wrap. If you've wrapped text around an image with a transparent backdrop, InDesign creates a path around the picture's border; if you've made a shape using the drawing tools, InDesign automatically wraps text around those pathways.

Ensure that the object utilizes the Wrap around Object Shape text wrap before continuing with the next instructions. (If not, click the Wrap around Object Shape button in the Text Wrap panel to apply text wrapping.)

Remember to choose "Detect Edges" when using

a transparent background picture.

Follow these steps to change the path around a picture with text wrapping using the Direct Selection tool:

1. With the direct selection tool, choose the item.

The picture is picked up, and the path around the item is seen.

2. Using the Direct Selection tool, choose one of the anchor points on the text wrap path; then click and drag the selected point.

The route is altered based on how the point is moved. As soon as you modify the route around an item, the text wrapping instantly adapts.

3. Choose the Remove Anchor Point tool from the Tools panel to remove an existing anchor point.

Again, the route varies, and the text wrapping around the item adapts appropriately.

The offset settings in the Text Wrap panel may also be used to establish the distance between the wrapping text and the object's edge. Just raise the values to move the text farther from the border of the object.

Use of Pages and the Pages Panel

The page is the core component of any publication; it is where the visible content is developed. Important components of working with InDesign include page navigation and management. The Pages panel enables you to choose, modify, relocate, and traverse pages within a publication. When you select the default options, pages are made as facing pages, meaning they are formatted as two-page pairs, or spreads.

Otherwise, each page is formatted independently.

Whether a page is part of a spread or appears as a single page in the Pages panel is defined when you create a new document and may be modified in the Document Setup window.

The Pages panel, which can be accessed by selecting WindowPages, also allows you to add new pages to the document, duplicate pages, remove a page, or alter its size. Figure 3-8 depicts the pages panel, which consists of two primary sections: the (upper) master pages section and the (lower) part holding the document's pages.

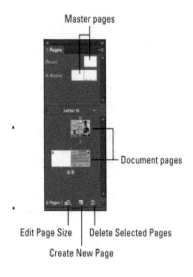

Master pages

Document pages

Edit Page Size | Delete Selected Pages
Create New Page

To learn more about master pages and how they vary from ordinary pages in your document, go to the section titled "Using Master Spreads in Page Layout" further in this text.

Choosing and rearranging pages

Choose a page or spread from your magazine using the Pages panel. To choose a page, just click the page. If you Ctrl-click (Windows) or -click (Mac) on several pages, you may pick multiple pages simultaneously. The Pages panel also allows you to reorder pages inside the document: Pick a page from the document pages section of the panel, and then drag it to the desired location. A thin line and a modified cursor show the location where the page will be relocated. You may move a page between two pages in a spread; a hollow line marks the location of the page movement. If a page is turned after a spread, a solid line will emerge. After the mouse button is released, the page will move to the new place.

Adding and removing pages

Moreover, you may add additional pages to the publication using the Pages panel. Follow these procedures to insert a new page:

1. Choose WindowPages to display the Pages panel.

Opens the Pages panel.

2. Click the icon labeled Create New Page.

The addition of a new page to the manuscript.

Alt-click (Windows) or Option-click (Mac OS) the Create New Page button to choose the number of pages to add and their location.

3. Choose a page from the Pages panel.

The marked page appears in the Pages panel.

4. Repeatedly click the Create New Page button.

The chosen page is followed by a new page.

To remove a page, click the Delete Selected Pages button after selecting it in the Pages window. Removes the specified page from the document.

You may also create, remove, and relocate pages without the Pages panel by selecting LayoutPages from the drop-down menu.

Numbering your pages

When dealing with lengthy papers, it is advisable to include page numbers before printing or exporting the publication. You do not need to add them manually. A unique InDesign function allows you to automatically number pages.

This tool is very handy for moving pages inside a document.

While making these changes, you do not need to keep track of the numbers.

To add page numbers, follow these steps:

1. Create a text frame on the page where you want the page number to appear using the Type tool.
2. From the Type menu, select TypeInsert Special CharacterMarkersC

urrent   Page
Number.

The current page number
is shown in the chosen
text frame. If the page
number was added to a
master page, the letter of
the master page will
appear in the field.

Add the text frame to a
master page if you want
page numbers to show on
all pages of the document.
Keep in mind that page
numbers are only assigned
to the pages of your
document that correspond
to the master page. To add
page numbers to the left
and right sides of a book
or magazine, this
technique must be
repeated on the left and

right sides of the master
pages. Recall that if you
add a page number just to
a document page and not
to the master, the page
number will only be
updated for that page.

Select LayoutNumbering
and Section Settings to
change the settings for
automatic numbering. You
have the option of using
Roman numerals or a
specified starting number.

Use of Master Spreads within Page Layout

Master pages are quite
similar to the templates
used to construct page
layouts. Each layout to
which the master page is

applied inherits the parameters, such as margins and columns. If you include a page number on the master page, it appears on every page that employs the layout. You may include many master pages in a single publication, and you can choose which pages utilize each master page.

Often, a master page or spread comprises layout components that are applied to several pages. The master page has components that appear on several pages, such as page numbers, text frames for entering content, background pictures, and a headline that appears on every page. By default, you cannot modify the items on a master page on the pages it is allocated to; you can only edit them on the master page itself. To edit these master page components directly on a document page, you may override or even totally remove them. This capability is helpful for unique circumstances, such as altering the background of a single page in a document.

Master pages are lettered. By default, the first master page is the A-Master. By default, a second master page is known as the B-Master. When you establish a new publication, the A-Master will be applied to all of the first pages you open. You may add pages toward the end of the document that do not have a master page.

By making master pages and using them in your publication, you can create a format that can be used again and again. This can speed up the process of making publications with InDesign by a lot.

Developing a master layout

A document may need more than one master page or master spread. You may have additional pages that need a certain format. This circumstance requires the creation of a second master page. You may construct a master page or spread from any other page in the magazine, or you can create one from scratch using the Pages panel.

To construct a master page using a page from the magazine, choose one of the options below.

- ❖ Choose New Master from the menu of the Page window, and then click OK. Create a blank master page.
- ❖ Drape a page from the Pages panel's pages section into the master page

section. The first page of the document becomes the master page.

If the page you want to drag into the master pages area is part of a spread, you must first select both pages in the spread before dragging the page into the master pages section. Individual pages may only be dragged into the master page area if they are not part of a spread.

Applying, removing, and deleting master pages

You may apply a master page to a page after it has been created. Moreover, you may remove a page from a master page layout and erase a whole master page.

❖ To apply master page formatting to a publishing page or spread: Drag the desired master page from the master page part of the Pages panel onto the page you want to prepare in the document pages section. When the master page is dragged on top of the page, it has a thick outline. When you let go of the mouse when you see this outline, the formatting will be applied to the page.

❖ To delete a master page from a page in a document: Drag the None page from the master area of the Pages panel to the desired document page. You may need to use the scroll bar to locate the None page in the master pages section of the Pages panel.

❖ To remove a master page, select the undesirable page in the Pages panel, and then click Delete Master Page from the panel menu.

This operation deletes the master page permanently; it cannot be recovered. Therefore, think carefully before removing a master page.

Adjusting specific page sizes

With the Pages panel, you may adjust the size of individual pages inside a document, which is handy if one page is bigger than others and folds out. Instead, you may like to include a business card, an envelope, and a letterhead in a single document.

Follow these procedures to alter the page size of specific documents using the Pages panel:

1. In the Pages panel, click on the page you want to change.

2. Choose the new page size by clicking the Modify Page Size button at the bottom of the Pages screen.

3. Repeat the procedure for any more pages you want to change.

After adjusting the size of the pages, continue working on their design and layout as you normally would with any other page. The only distinction is that some of your document's pages may be of a different size.

Moreover, you may utilize the Pages panel to build alternate layouts for tablet devices.

Drawing in InDesign

You can draw lines and shapes on a page with several tools in the InDesign Tools panel. This gives you a lot of options for making interesting illustrations for your publications. You don't need a separate drawing program like Adobe Illustrator if you have InDesign. You can make anything from simple shapes to complex drawings. Even though it can't replace Illustrator, which has more drawing tools and options for making more complex designs, InDesign can do many drawing jobs well. This chapter shows you how to use the most common drawing tools in InDesign and how to fill pictures with color.

Even if you do not anticipate sketching with InDesign, you should review the sections under "Modifying Frame Corners" and "Using Fills."

How to Begin with Drawing

You might want to sketch shapes and paths into the layout of a document you are making. For instance, you may need a star shape for a page in a yearbook describing a talent event, or you may want to run text along a route. Whatever you need to do, you may do it by drawing shapes and pathways.

Routes and forms

There are several types of paths. They may be opened or closed, with or without a stroke.

❖ The form or thing's shape. Routes may be either closed with no gaps or open like a line on a page. You may easily draw freeform pathways by hand, such as squiggles on a page.

❖ A stroke is the line style and thickness applied to a route. A stroke may appear as either a line or the outline of a form.

Pathways include locations where the path's direction may be altered. (For more information on points, see the following section, "Points and Segments.")You can build routes by utilizing freeform drawing tools, such as the Pen or Pencil tools, or by using the fundamental shape tools, such as Ellipse, Rectangle, Polygon, or Line.

With the form tools, you can make simple geometric shapes like a star or an ellipse by building paths in a set way. All you need to do is select the shape tool and move the pointer on the page, and the shape is automatically created. This is a much easier way to make forms than using the Pen or Pencil tool by hand. In the picture below, you can see how to make shapes with the form tools in the Tools panel.

You may transform forms into freeform pathways

similar to those created with the pencil and pen tools. Similarly, it is possible to convert freeform routes into fundamental forms. Hence, you should not worry about the tool you choose first.

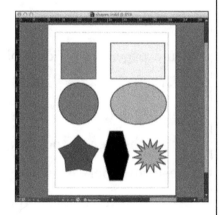

Segments and points

Pathways include points and segments:

❖ Point: The location where the journey alters in some way, such as a change in direction.

Using segments, several sites along a route may be connected.

Sometimes, points are referred to as anchor points. You are able to generate two types of points:

• There should be a straight line connecting the corner points. Squares and stars, among other shapes, have corner points.

• Curve points: points that appear along a curved route. Circular or serpentine pathways feature several curved points.

❖ A line or curve that connects two points; similar to connecting the dots.

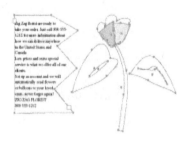

Understanding the Tools of the Trade

The sections that follow will expose you to the tools you will likely use most often while designing illustrations for your books. As you create designs using these tools,

you use strokes and fills. The next sections demonstrate how these standard InDesign tools may be used to create simple or complicated illustrations.

The Pencil Device

On a page, the pencil tool is used to create basic or complicated forms. Since the Pencil tool is a freeform tool, you may freely move it over the page to make lines or forms, as opposed to using basic shape tools that automatically construct them for you. The Pencil

tool is an easy-to-use and intuitive tool. You will

learn how to use it in the part titled "Drawing Freeform Paths."

The Pen Device

The pen tool is used to make intricate forms on the page. The Pen tool is compatible with tools such as Add, Delete, and Convert Point. By adding and altering points along a route, the Pen tool manipulates the segments that connect them.

Drawing using the Pen tool is initially challenging. In reality, it takes a great deal of effort for many individuals to master this instrument. Don't get irritated if it takes some time to become acclimated to the Pen tool; it might take some practice to get it to perform as desired. In the "Drawing Freeform Paths" module, you learn how to use the Pen tool.

Standard forms and frame shapes

With the tools in the Tools tab, you may add basic forms to a document as premade shapes. Line, rectangle, ellipse, and polygon are the basic form tools.

You may also transform these forms into frames (document containers that carry content). You may use a frame as either a text frame or a graphic frame to accommodate both text and images. Create a simple form and then choose ObjectContentText or ObjectContentGraphic to convert it to a graphic or text frame, respectively.

The frame and shape tools seem identical and may even function identically. Both may include text and photos, but beware! By default, forms made using the shape tools are surrounded by a 1-point black stroke. Many individuals do not see these strokes on the screen but find them while printing. Use just the frame tools, and you will be alright.

Drawing Shapes

InDesign allows the creation of simple shapes inside a document. Creating a simple form is simple if you follow these steps:

1. Create a brand-new document by selecting FileNew.
2. Click OK when the New Document dialog box opens. A new document opens.
3. On the Tools panel, choose the rectangle tool.
4. Click anywhere on the page and diagonally drag the mouse.

After the rectangle has reached the desired size, release the mouse button. You have fashioned a rectangle.

That is all that is required to build a simple form. These methods may also be used with the Line, Ellipse, and Polygon tools to build more basic forms. Follow these procedures to access the other basic shapes in the Tools panel:

1. Click and hold the mouse button on the rectangle tool. A menu including all the fundamental forms is shown.
2. Let go of the mouse button.

The menu stays open, and you may hover your cursor over its contents.

3. When the mouse cursor is put over a menu item, that item gets highlighted.

Click the highlighted menu item to choose a basic form tool.

Active is the new basic shape tool. Using any of these tools, make simple shapes by following the previous stages.

Use the rectangle tool and the Shift key while dragging the mouse over the page to create a square. The shape's sides are all drawn at the same length, resulting in a perfect square. If you want to create a perfect circle using the Ellipse tool, you may also hold down the Shift key while using the tool. Remove the mouse before pressing Shift to guarantee that this limit-form technique is effective.

Designing a form using precise measurements

Creating a form by dragging on the page is simple, but creating a shape with accurate proportions needs additional steps. Follow these instructions if you'd like to create a form of a certain size:

1. Choose either the rectangle or ellipse tool.
   The highlighted tool is located in the Tools panel.

2. Click anywhere on the page without dragging the pointer.
   This point becomes the upper-left corner of the rectangle or ellipse bounding box (the rectangle defining the vertical and horizontal dimensions of the item). After

selecting a corner, the Rectangle or Ellipse dialog box will display.

3. Enter the measurements for constructing the form in the Width and Height text areas.

4. Click the Accept button.

   The form is produced on the page, with the upper-left corner located at the original point of click.

Using the polygon apparatus

A polygon is a shape composed of several sides. For instance, a square is a polygon with four sides, but the Polygon tool allows you to choose the number of sides for the newly created polygon. You may not want to build a form with the default number of sides when using the polygon tool.

You may modify these parameters before beginning to design the shape. Follow the instructions below to modify the form of a polygon.

1. Choose the polygon tool from the Tools panel by holding down the mouse button while choosing the rectangle tool.
2. Click the Polygon tool twice in the Tools panel.

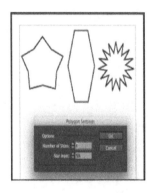

3. Enter the desired number of sides in the "Number of Sides" text area the latest polygon to own.

To build a star instead of a polygon, put a value in the "Star Inset" text box according to the desired percentage of star inset for the new design.

A higher percentage indicates that the sides of the polygon are recessed more toward the center, making a star. Enter 0 in the Star Inset text area if you want a normal polygon and not a star. If you want a star, enter 50%; otherwise, put 25%.

4. Click the Accept button.

5. Click and drag on the page to form a new polygon or star.

Your new polygon or star is now shown on the website.

Editing Standard Shapes

InDesign allows you to alter basic forms using several panels, allowing you to construct original shapes and make precisely the page layout design you need. You are not limited to specified forms like squares and ovals. These formations may take on much more intricate or unique shapes.

There are just a few methods to alter simple shapes in InDesign. You can modify forms and alters their appearance in many ways. We discuss some of these methods, such as modifying fills, in the section titled "Using Fills."

Adjusting the size of the panel Transform

The Transform panel allows you to adjust the size of a shape. This is how:

1. Choose the desired shape using the selection tool (the solid black arrow

that is used to select items).

A bounding box appears around the shape when it is chosen.

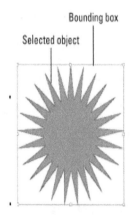

Bounding box

Selected object

2. Choose WindowObject and LayoutTransform to open the Transform panel.

3. In the resulting Transform panel, enter various numbers in the W and H fields to adjust the size of the shape.

The size of the shape is automatically adjusted to the new parameters specified in the Transform tab.

Size modification with the Free Transform tool

Use InDesign's Free Transform tool to quickly resize items.

Follow these steps to resize a chosen item using the Free Transform tool:

1. Ensure that just the item you want to

resize is chosen before proceeding.

If you wish to resize numerous items concurrently, group them. To group items, pick one and Shift-click to add it to the selection, then press Ctrl+G (Windows) or +G (Mac OS X) (Mac).

2. Choose the Free Transform instrument.

3. Click and drag any corner point to resize the item.

Hold down the Shift key while dragging to maintain proportionality as you resize things.

Altering the shape's stroke

You may alter the stroke of the shapes you've made. The stroke is the contour around the perimeter of a form. It is assessed in point sizes and may vary from no stroke to an extremely thick stroke. Even if a shape's stroke is set to o points, it still has one; it's simply invisible.

Use these procedures to modify your forms' strokes:

1. Choose a shape from the page.

A box emerges around the specified form.

2. Using the Stroke Weight drop-down menu in the Control panel, choose a new width for the Stroke.

As soon as a value is picked, the stroke on the page changes automatically. This quantity is expressed in points. You choose one or more of the alternatives from the subsequent step list.

You may manually input a number value for the stroke width by clicking on the Stroke text area. The thickness of the stroke increases as the number entered increases. You may also modify the stroke style from the Control panel using the following steps:

1. With a basic form chosen, choose the stroke type from the Control panel's drop-down menu and choose a new line.

As soon as a value is chosen, the stroke changes automatically.

2. Select a different line weight from the Stroke Weight drop-down menu. For instance, we choose 10 points.

The website automatically refreshes the form.

If you wish to make bespoke dashes, choose WindowStroke for further possibilities. Choose Stroke Styles from the panel menu in the upper-right corner of the panel, and then create a new style. You may set the size of dashes and spaces. Input a single value for an even dash or several values for customized dashes on maps, diagrams, fold marks, and more! After creating a custom stroke, it displays in the Stroke panel.

With the Start and Finish drop-down menus, you may customize the line ends. For instance, an arrowhead or a huge circle may be added at the beginning or finish of the stroke. When dealing with complicated routes or forms, the Cap and Join buttons enable you to pick the shape of the line ends and how they combine with other paths.

Modifying shear value

With the Transform panel, you may modify a shape's shear. Skew and shear have the same meaning: the slanted shape creates the impression of perspective for the skewed or sheared part.

This transition is helpful for creating the appearance of depth on a webpage.

To skew a form, just do the following steps:

1. Choose a simple shape and go to WindowObject & LayoutTransform.

2. Select a value from the Shear drop-down menu in the Transform panel's lower-right corner. When selecting a new value, the shape skews (or shears) based on the selected value.

Inputting a value manually into this field also distorts the form.

Rotating a form

The Transform panel enables you to modify the rotation of a shape. Rotating a shape is analogous to skewing a shape (refer to the previous section):

1. Choose a simple shape and go to WindowObject & LayoutTransform. The panel for Transform opens.

2. Select a value from the drop-down menu labeled Rotation.

When selecting a new value, the form rotates automatically depending on the selected rotation angle. You may also input a value directly into the text area.

Creating Free-Form Routes

Several tools may be used to draw pathways. With the Pencil tool, for instance, you may create freeform pathways. These types of routes often resemble lines, and the Pencil and Pen tools may be used to build basic or complicated paths.

Using the pencil device

The pencil tool is the most intuitive tool for sketching freeform pathways.

Follow the steps below to begin:

1. To create a new document, click OK in the New Document dialog box that opens after selecting FileNew.

2. Choose the pencil tool from the Tools panel.

3. Move the pointer across the page. With the pencil tool, you've produced a new route.

Using the Pen Tool

Using the pen tool is distinct from employing the pencil tool. The Pen tool may seem sophisticated at first, but once you get the feel of it, it's really rather simple to use. The Pen tool creates a specific route using points. These points may be edited to modify the segments between them.

Acquiring command of these points may take some practice.

Follow the instructions below to add points and segments to a page:

1. Close any open documents and create a new document by selecting File > New Document.

2. Click OK in the resulting New Document dialog box. The default settings are applied to a new document.

3. Choose the pencil tool from the Tools panel.

4. Click anywhere on the page, followed by another position.

   You have generated a new route consisting of two points with a segment connecting them.

5. Ctrl-click (Windows) or -click (Mac) on a blank area of the page to deselect the current route.

   After deselecting a route, you may build a new path or add additional points to the newly-created path.

6. Add a new point to a segment by placing the mouse pointer above the line and clicking.

   A little addition (+) symbol appears next to the cursor of the Pen tool. You can also accomplish the same result by choosing the Add Anchor Point tool from the menu that appears when you click and hold the Pen icon in the Tools panel.

7. Repeat Step 6, but this time click a different position on a line segment and drag in the opposite direction of the line.

This action forms a curved route. Depending on the location of the points along the route, the segments shift and curve. The produced point is a curve point.

Changes to Freeform Pathways

Even the finest artists must sometimes make adjustments or eliminate portions of their work. Follow the instructions in this section to make modifications to a drawing if you've made errors or changed your mind.

To modify a section of a route, choose a point using the Direct Selection tool. Unselected spots seem hollow, whereas chosen points appear solid. To choose the direct selection tool, hit the A button.

To choose a point, you only need to click the point with the pointer.

When a point is chosen, handles appear that can be used to change the segments. Follow the instructions below:

1. Click a point after selecting the Direct Selection tool from the Tools menu.
   The chosen point is solid-looking.
   When a curve point

is selected, handles extend from it.

When dragged, a curved point and a corner point are edited differently. Corner points do not have handles extending from the point, but curve points do.

2. Move the point to the desired location; to adjust a curve point, click an end handle and slide it left or right. The route varies depending on how the handles are dragged.

Imagine you want to transform a corner point into a curve point. This is possible using the Convert Direction Point tool. For the greatest understanding of how the Convert Direction Point tool works, a route including both straight and curved portions is required. To convert a corner point to a curved point and vice versa, follow these steps:

1. Choose the Convert Direction Point instrument.

This tool is accessible via a submenu of the Pen tool in the Tools panel. Select the Convert Direction Point tool from the menu that appears when you hover your mouse over the Pen tool icon.

2. Using the Convert Direction Point tool, click a curved point.

The place you click becomes a corner point, altering the look of the route.

3. Clicking and dragging a corner point with the Convert Direction Point tool is required.

The point is altered to become a curved point. This stage modifies the path's look once again. This tool is useful for modifying the way a route changes direction. If you need to manage a point differently, you may need to use the Change Direction Point tool to alter its type.

Altering the frame's corners

You may change the appearance of simple forms with corner effects. Corner effects are excellent for enhancing the visual appeal of borders. You may be fairly inventive when adding effects to certain forms or when applying many effects to a single shape.

Here's how to give a rectangle rounded corners:

1. With the Rectangle tool, draw a new rectangle on the page.
   If you wish to construct a square using the Rectangle tool, hold down the Shift key.

2. Pick the shape using the Selection tool, and then click Object > Corner Options.
   Opens the Corner Options dialog box.

3. Choose the desired corner type, then click OK.
   The shape's corner choice is applied.

Select a frame with the Selection tool to change the corner effects visually. Click the yellow box that appears at the top right border of the frame when it is chosen. After clicking the yellow box, each corner handle becomes yellow and may be moved horizontally to create rounded corners.

Using Fills

A fill is placed within a route. You may fill pathways and objects with a variety of colors, including transparent colors and gradients. Fills may be used to create artistic effects and illusions of depth or to add visual interest to a website layout.

You may have previously made a fill. The Tools panel has two color swatches:

One for the hollow square stroke and one for the square fill (a solid box). If the Fill box includes a color, your form will be produced with a fill. If the Fill box is highlighted in red, the shape will be built without a fill

Generating standard fills

Creating a simple fill may be done in several ways. One of the most common methods for creating a new shape is to specify a color in the Fill swatch.

To construct a shape with a fill, do the following steps:

1. Ensure that the Fill checkbox is checked so that color is not added to the stroke.
2. To access the Color Panel, choose WindowColorColor

.

3. Choose a color from the Color Panel.

You can use the sliders or type numbers into the Cyan, Magenta, Yellow, and Black (CMYK) boxes. Instead, you may choose a color from the color ramp at the bottom of the Color panel by using the Eyedropper tool.

If CMYK is not already chosen, use the Color Panel's menu to pick other color modes. Choose CMYK from the Color Panel menu by pressing and holding the arrow button.

The new color picked in the Color panel is applied to the Fill box in the Tools panel.

4. Add a new shape to the page.

Choose a shape tool and drag it around the page to create a shape.

The shape is filled with the color chosen for the fill. Like with other Creative Cloud programs, you may create tints of CMYK-based colors by holding the Shift key while sliding the slider for any hue. Then, each color slider will shift correspondingly.

With the Swatches panel, you may also pick a fill color using color swatches. Choose WindowColorSwatches to access the Swatches panel. Clicking the "New Swatch" button at the bottom of the panel will create a new color swatch (of the current color). Double-click the new swatch to add additional color attributes by setting CMYK color values using the sliders or by entering numbers in each text box.

You may already have a form without a fill and want to add one, or you may wish to alter the color of an existing fill. Choose the shape and, in the Tools panel's Fill box, choose a color from the Color or Swatches panels. The fill color of the shape is changed. Even if a shape is not chosen, it is possible to drag and drop a color swatch to fill it. Activate the Swatches panel by selecting WindowColorSwatches, and then drag the color swatch onto the shape. When the mouse button is released, the fill color is immediately applied to the shape.

Creating transparent fills

Partially transparent fills might provide some fascinating effects for your document's layout. You may apply transparency to many page components and stack them to create the appearance of depth and stacking.

Follow these procedures to add transparency to a page element:

1. Using the Selection tool, choose a page-based shape.

   A box emerges around the specified form.

2. Access the Effects panel by selecting WindowEffects from the Window menu.

3. Use the Opacity slider to set the degree of transparency of the form.

   Click the arrow to open the slider, or click the text box to input a value manually using the keyboard. The effect is applied instantly to the specified form.

4. Select Stroke or Fill in the Effects tab to assign each a distinct opacity.

Looking at gradients

A gradient is the change of color from one color (or no color) to another. There may be two or more colors in a gradient's transition.

Gradients may provide forms with intriguing effects, including 3D effects.

Gradients may sometimes be used to generate glowing effects or the appearance of light striking a surface. The two gradient types accessible in InDesign are radial and linear, as detailed in the following list:

- ❖ Radial: A circular transition of colors from a central point spreading outward.
- ❖ Linear: A progression of hues along a linear line

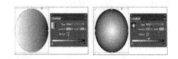

Gradients may be applied to strokes, fills, and even text. Choose the stroke instead of the fill to apply a gradient to a stroke.

Even while it is possible to add a gradient to the stroke of live text, you will create a printing nightmare if you utilize these capabilities often.

Here's how to fill a shape with a gradient:

1. Choose the item to which you want to apply a gradient using the Selection tool, and then go to WindowColorSwatches.

   Opens the Swatches panel.

2. Choose New Gradient Swatch in the Swatches panel menu.

   Opens the New Gradient Swatch dialog box.

3. Rename the swatch in the Swatch Name field.

   Sometimes it is good to give the swatch a descriptive name, such as one that indicates the purpose of the swatch.

4. From the Type drop-down menu, choose Linear or Radial.

   This option controls the kind of gradient created each time the swatch is used. We picked Radial from the list of options.

5. Modify the gradient stops under the

Gradient Ramp to place each color inside the gradient. Gradient stops are the color chips underneath the Gradient Ramp. You may drag the diamond shape above the Gradient Ramp to adjust the gradient's center. You may adjust the gradient by changing the color of each gradient stop and rearranging them. After the gradient stops are chosen, you may modify the color values in the Stop Color box using the sliders or text fields for CMYK.

Clicking the region between gradient stops will allow you to add a new color to the gradient. Afterwards, the new stop may be edited similarly to the others. Drag the gradient stop away from the Gradient Ramp to remove it.

6. Choose OK.

Create and apply the gradient swatch to the specified item.

Double-click the gradient's swatch to modify it. This action launches the Gradient

Options dialogue box, where you may adjust the parameters established in the Create Gradient Swatch dialog box.

Removing fills

The removal of fillings is even simpler than their creation. Follow the instructions below:

1. With the Selection tool, choose the shape.

   A bounding box emerges around the shape.

2. Choose the Fill checkbox from the Tools panel.

3. Click the Apply None button under the Fill box.

The button is white with a red dividing line. The chosen shape's fill is deleted, and the Fill box is changed to No Fill. The None fill also appears in the Swatches and Color panels.

If you are using a single-row Tools panel, the Apply None button is not shown until you press and hold the Apply Gradient (or Apply Color) button.

Adding Layers

Similar to translucent sheets layered on top of one another, layers resemble transparent sheets. By adding layers to a design, it is possible to simulate the look of visuals layered on top of one another. The Layers panel enables you to add new layers, eliminate unnecessary levels, and even rearrange layers to alter their stacking order. You may even clone an InDesign file and then add or delete layers to generate a new document version.

Here's how to deal with InDesign layers:

1. To access the Layers panel, choose WindowLayers.

This panel permits the creation, deletion, and arrangement of layers.

2. Use a shape tool to create a form on the page.

Make the shape anywhere on the page and make it big enough so that it may be stacked on top of another form.

3. To create a new layer, click the Create New Layer button in the Layers window.

A new layer is added on top of the existing layer and becomes active.

Double-click a layer to rename it, or better yet, hold the Alt (Windows) or Option (Mac) key and click the Create Layer button to access the Layer Settings dialog box before to creating the layer.

Ensure that the layer on which you want to generate content is chosen before to changing it. The chosen layer is always highlighted in the Layers window, so you can determine which one is active. If you do not routinely check this

panel, you may easily yet mistakenly upload material to the wrong layer. You can always cut and paste objects to the right layer if you mistakenly add them to the incorrect layer.

4. Ensure that the form tool is still active, and then build a shape on the new layer by moving the cursor such that a portion of the newly produced shape overlaps the previously created shape.

The new form is placed on the previously-created shape.

Developing QR Codes

You may generate and change QR code graphics with InDesign. QR codes are a kind of barcode that may hold text, numbers, URLs, and other types of information. The user scans the QR code using the camera and software on a device, such as a smartphone, and the program utilizes the encoded data; for instance, it opens a browser with the encoded URL, identifies a product, tracks a shipment, etc. You may encode hyperlinks, text, text messages, email messages, and business cards using InDesign.

InDesign interprets QR codes as images, so you can resize them and alter their colors just as you would with other artwork in your pages. These can even be copied and pasted into Illustrator!

With InDesign, you add a QR code to an empty frame. Follow these procedures to include an image in a document:

1. Click and drag the Rectangle Frame tool to create an

empty frame on the page.

2. Choose your new frame, then click Object > Create QR Code.

   With the Content tab selected, the Create QR Code dialog box displays.

3. Choose the data type to encode from the Type option.

   Choose from Web Hyperlink, Plain Text, Text Message, Email, and a Business Card.

   Depending on the Type you choose, the space below this option will change accordingly.

4. Input the information to be encoded in the QR code.

   The space underneath the Type menu is populated with text fields for data entry. For instance, if you choose email, you must provide an address, topic, and message. Alternatively, if you choose a business card, you must provide your name, organization, addresses, etc.

5. Choose a color swatch by clicking the Color tab.

This determines the color of your QR code, which impacts how it appears on the website. After inserting the QR code on the website, you may change the color by modifying the Fill and Stroke characteristics of the chosen frame.

6. Choose OK.

The QR code is added to the frame that was chosen. If more editing is required, choose the text frame and select ObjectEdit QR Code.

Understanding Color

Color may play a vital role in the designs you develop. Advertisements often depend on color to convey brands or effective messages; consider the package delivery firm whose logo is brown or the soft drink company whose cans are red. Color may enhance your message and, when utilized consistently, contribute to the development of a brand identity. Whether you're printing or creating electronic documents, you want color to show right when you use it. In this chapter, you will learn the fundamentals of working with color and how to prepare files for printing.

Color Selection Using Color Controls

With InDesign, there are several color modes and settings from which to pick. This section describes how to use the Color Panel to choose colors and apply them to page components.

This shows you how to save color swatches so that you can use them again and again.

You should use swatches whenever possible because they have specific colors that a service provider can match exactly. A swatch may have the exact same look as any color you choose that is nameless, but a swatch provides a connection between the color on the page and a color name, such as a Pantone color number. Learn more about these hues in the section under "Using Color Swatches and Libraries."

These color controls may be used to choose colors for document selections:

❖ Stroke color: Select colors for InDesign strokes and pathways. A box with no inside symbolizes the stroke color control.
❖ Fill color: choose colors to use for filling in shapes.

The fill color is shown as a solid square box.

By clicking the Fill and Stroke color settings, you may switch between them. You can also switch between controls by pressing X on the keyboard.

❖ Text color: A separate color control becomes active when dealing with text. The text color slider is displayed and shows the color of the chosen text. Both the stroke and fill of text may be colored.

Click the Apply color button underneath the color settings in the Tools panel to apply colors to your choices. Instead, you may choose a color swatch and click it.

In InDesign, the default colors are a black stroke with no fill color. Press D to restore the default colors at any moment. This shortcut works for all tools except the type tool.

Understanding Color Models

InDesign supports three different color models: CMYK (cyan, magenta, yellow, black), RGB (red, green, blue), and LAB (lightness and A and B for the color-opposite dimensions of the color space). A color model is a method that represents each color as a series of numbers or characters (or both). The optimal color model depends on how you want to print or show the content:

- ❖ Use the RGB color model when preparing a PDF that will be delivered online and likely not be printed. RGB is how a computer monitor displays colors.
- ❖ When dealing with process colors, the CMYK color model

must be used. Instead of having inks that precisely match certain hues, four ink colors are blended to imitate a specific hue. Remember that the colors seen on the monitor may vary from those written on the document. Sample swatch books and numbers may assist you in determining which colors to use in a document to match the final printed colors.

- ❖ If professionals who will determine what each color is before printing will print the document, it doesn't matter if you use CMYK, RGB, or Pantone colors. In many cases, CMYK colors show what will be printed more accurately, while RGB colors are usually more vivid and bright on your screen.

Use of Color Samples and Libraries

You can choose, save, and use colors in your documents with the help of the Swatches panel and swatch libraries. A document's color scheme might vary widely. For instance, one publication you create using InDesign may be a newsletter with simply two colors, while another may be a catalog with CMYK and a spot color. Customize the available swatches for each document so that you can work more effectively.

The Swatches section

The Swatches panel enables you to generate, apply, and modify colors. In addition to creating and editing tints and gradients and applying them to items on a page, you can also generate and save solid colors with this panel. Choose WindowColorSwatches to expand or contract the Swatches panel.

Follow these procedures to generate a new color swatch for use in a document:

1. Choose a new color swatch from the Swatches panel menu by clicking the arrow situated in the upper-right corner of the Swatches panel. Opens the New Color Swatch dialog box.

2. You can give the color swatch a new name or leave it as is, with its color values.

By default, the Swatches panel refers to the colors by their respective color values. The chosen name is shown alongside the color swatch when it is put into the panel.

3. Choose the desired hue from the Color Type drop-down menu. Use a spot color, such as Pantone, or process color, which is utilized when printing with cyan, magenta, yellow, and black (CMYK)?

4. Choose the color mode.

Choose a color option from the Color Mode drop-down menu. In this example, CMYK is used. Several further options include prebuilt color libraries for different platforms.

5. Create the desired color with the color sliders.

Notice that if you begin with black, you must move this slider to the left in order to view the other colors.

If you pick a spot color, such as Pantone, you will be provided with a collection of color swatches rather than the color sliders.

6. Press OK or Add.

Click Add if you want to add more colors to the Swatches panel, or click OK if this is the only color you wish to add. Add the color or colors to the Swatches panel. After you've finished adding color swatches, click OK if you chose Add.

Changes to the swatch may be made by selecting it in the Swatches panel and selecting Swatch Options from the panel menu, or by double-clicking it in the Swatches panel.

Swatch collections

Swatch libraries, also known as color libraries, are standardized collections of color swatches that are frequently used. You may skip mixing your own colors, which can be difficult or time-consuming to do correctly. InDesign, for instance, has a swatch library for Pantone spot colors and a separate swatch library for Pantone process colors. If you're dealing with either color palette, these libraries are highly handy. If you missed it, you may want to study the section "Understanding Color Models" where the distinction between spot and process colors is explained.

To choose a swatch from a swatch library, do the following steps:

1. Choose a new color swatch from the options in the Swatches panel. Opens the New Color Swatch dialog box.

2. Choose the color type you want to use from the Color Type drop-down menu.

Choose between Process and Spot Colors.

3. Choose a color palette from the Color Mode drop-down menu.

   The drop-down menu provides a selection of color swatch libraries, including Pantone Process Coated and TRUMATCH.

   When a swatch set is selected, the library opens and displays in the dialogue box.We picked ordinary, solid-coated Pantone for this example. If you're searching for the conventional numerical Pantone colors, this package offers the most options. The Pantone solid-coated swatch collection is packed.

4. Choose a fabric swatch from the collection.

   If you have a Pantone number, enter it in the Pantone text box. The majority of businesses use Pantone colors for uniformity. You may also browse and choose a color swatch from the library's list of hues.

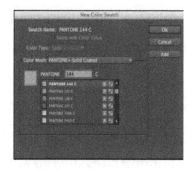

It is difficult to choose Pantone colors with a color monitor. Your monitor does not display colors in their most true form or as they will appear when printed. If you want to print your document in large quantities or if color is crucial, we recommend acquiring a Pantone color swatch book, such as the Pantone Color Bridge Set. For further information on this guide, please visit www.pantone.com and search for Color Bridge.

5. Press the "Add" button.

This step adds the swatch to the Swatches panel's collection of color swatches. You are permitted to upload as many color samples as you like.

6. After adding swatches is complete, click the OK button.

After adding a new color, the swatch is added to the swatches panel's list of swatches and is available for usage in your project. The newly added colors may be seen in the swatches tab.

Clipping Paths, Alignment, and Object Transformation

You learn several techniques for manipulating and arranging items on a page. You learn how to manipulate items on page layouts using the Transform panel and other Tools panel capabilities. There are other methods to do the same transformation in InDesign; thus, for each method of object transformation, we demonstrate two alternatives.

Aligning and distributing objects and pictures facilitates the logical organization of page components. It demonstrates how to align items using the Align panel. We demonstrate how to generate a new clipping path for a picture in your document.

Using Transformations

InDesign allows you to alter elements in several more ways.

You can modify an item by selecting it and utilizing the Transform panel, accessible through WindowObject & LayoutTransform, or by using the Free Transform tool to alter things visually.

Looking at the panel Transform

The Transform panel is very handy for altering the appearance of an image or graphic, as well as the size, rotation, and skew of selected objects. You may pick from a variety of values for some of these modifiers, or you can type in your own.

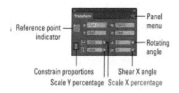

The Transform panel provides the following data and features:

❖ Reference point: Specifies which handle is used as a point of reference for modifications. For instance, if the X and Y coordinates are reset, the reference point is set to this location.

❖ Position: Modify these values to reset the chosen object's X and Y coordinates.

❖ Size: The W and H text boxes are used to modify the object's current size.

❖ Scale: Input or choose a percentage from

the Scale X% and Scale Y% drop-down menus to scale the item along one of these axes.

❖ Constraining proportions: Click the "Constrain Proportions" button to keep the scaled object's present proportions.

❖ Input a negative or positive value to adjust the shearing angle (skew) of the chosen item.

❖ Set a negative number for clockwise rotation and a positive value for counterclockwise rotation.

As you scale, shear, or rotate an item in your layout, the object transforms according to the reference point in the Transform panel. When you rotate an item, for instance, InDesign considers the reference point to be the rotation's center.

Clicking a new reference point square in the Transform panel will change the graphic's reference point to the bounding box handle of the chosen item.

Using the Free Transform device

The versatile Free Transform tool permits many object transformations. With the Free Transform tool, objects may be translated, rotated, sheared, reflected, and scaled.

Rotate   Scale   Scale   Move

Follow these steps to move an item using the Free Transform tool:

1. Use the selection tool to choose a page element.

   You may use an existing item on the page or design a new form utilizing the drawing tools. When an item is chosen, handles appear around its perimeter.

2. From the Tools panel, choose the Free Transform tool.

   The cursor is now positioned above the Free Transform tool.

3. Position the pointer in the center of the chosen item.

   The look of the pointer changes to show that you may drag to move an item. When additional tools, such as rotate, scale, and shear, become active, the cursor changes when it leaves the object's borders.

4. Move the item to a new spot by dragging it.

The item gets relocated to a different position on the page.

Revolving objects

Use the Free Transform tool, the rotate tool, or the Transform panel to rotate an item. Use the panel to specify the desired degree of rotation for the item. The Free Transform tool allows for the visual manipulation of page objects.

Follow these instructions to rotate a picture using the Free Transform tool:

1. Using the selection tool, choose an item from the page. Handles appear at the object's edges. You are able to rotate any element on the page.

2. Choose the Free Transform tool from the Tools panel and position it close to the object's handle outside the bounding box.

The cursor changes when it is brought near an object's handle.

3. To rotate an item, you must maintain the pointer just outside of it.

As the pointer changes to the "rotate" cursor, drag the item to rotate it.

Move the cursor until the item is rotated appropriately.

Instead, you may rotate an object with the Rotate tool by following these steps:

1. With the object chosen, pick the Rotate tool from the Tools panel by clicking and holding the arrow in the lower-right corner of the Free Transform tool, then dragging the mouse close to the object.

The cursor resembles a pair of crosshairs.

2. Click anywhere on the page close to the item.

The point around which the item revolves is specified on the page.

3. Move the cursor away from the thing.

The item revolves around the specified reference point on the page. If you wish to rotate in 45-degree increments, hold down the Shift key.

Objects may also be rotated using the Transform panel. This is how:

1. Using the selection tool, choose an item from the page. A box with handles emerges around the chosen item.

2. If the Transform panel is not already visible, choose WindowObject and LayoutTransform. The Transform panel is shown.

3. Choose a number from the Rotation Angle drop-down box or enter a percentage in the text field.

The item will rotate to the degree you choose in the Transform tab.

Positive angles (in degrees) spin the picture counterclockwise, whereas negative angles (in degrees) rotate it clockwise.

Object scalability

Objects may be scaled using the Transform panel, the Scale tool, or the Free Transform tool. Provide the precise width and height dimensions to which you wish to scale the item in the Transform panel, just as you may select specific percentages for rotating.

Follow these steps to scale an item using the Free Transform or Scale tools:

1. Choose an item from the page.
   The thing is surrounded by a bounding box.
2. From the Tools panel, choose the Free Transform or Scale tools.
3. Place the cursor over a corner handle.
   The cursor becomes a double-ended arrow.
4. Move the thing outward to make it bigger; drag it inside to make it smaller.
   Hold down the Shift key while dragging to resize the picture appropriately.
5. After the item has been scaled to the proper size, release the mouse button.

To resize an item, select it and enter new values into the W and H text areas in the Transform panel. The item is then resized to those precise measurements.

Objects being sheared

Shearing anything implies skewing it horizontally,

slanting it to the left or right. Because of this alteration, a sheared object may seem to have perspective or depth.

To shear an item, follow these steps:

1. Choose an item from the page.
   The bounding box appears around the selected item.

2. In the Tools panel, choose the shear tool by clicking and holding the Free Transform tool.
   The cursor transforms into the shape of a crosshair. When you click the corner of the item you want to shear from, a cross-hair appears.

3. Drag from anyplace above or below the item.
   The selected item shears depending on which way you drag it. Shift-drag an item in 45-degree increments by holding down the Shift key.

To shear objects using the Free Transform tool, drag a handle while holding down Ctrl+Alt (Windows) or +Option (Mac).

You may also delete an item by entering a precise value into the Transform window. Choose the item, then enter a positive or negative number in the panel to signify the amount of slant you wish to apply to it.

You may use shear by selecting ObjectTransformShear to open the Shear dialog box.

Objects that reflect

Using the Transform panel option, you may reflect items to create mirror images. The menu has a number of extra choices for manipulating objects.

To reflect an item, follow these steps:

1. Choose WindowObject & LayoutTransform from the Window menu, or choose an object on the page to launch the Transform panel.

   The bounding box and handles of the item display. The Transform tab displays the chosen object's current values.

2. On the Transform panel, click the panel menu.

   The menu appears, offering a plethora of possibilities for modifying the item.

3. From the Transform panel

menu, choose "Flip Horizontal."

The thing on the page flips horizontally. This procedure may be repeated with different reflection choices in the menu, such as Flip Vertical.

You may also use the Free Transform tool to reflect items by dragging a corner handle beyond the opposite end of the object. On its axis, the item reflects

Recognizing clipping paths

Clipping paths enable you to design a path that crops a portion of a picture depending on the path, such as deleting an image's backdrop. This shape may be created in InDesign or imported from an image that already contains a clipping path. InDesign may also treat an existing alpha or mask layer, such as one made in Photoshop or Fireworks, as a clipping path. Clipping paths may be used to block off portions of a picture and have text wrap around the remaining image.

A clipping path may be created directly in InDesign by using a drawing tool, such as the Pen tool. You construct a shape using the tool and then put an image into it on the page. If you anticipate reusing the clipping path and picture in the future, construct the path in Photoshop and save it as part of the image instead.

Here's an easy approach to removing an image's backdrop in InDesign:

1. Choose FilePlace and browse to find and open a picture.
2. Using the Pen tool, draw a path directly on top of the picture. The route should be established in such a way that it can hold the picture.
3. Using the Selection tool, select the image and then Edit Cut.
4. Choose "Edit/Paste Into" after selecting the form you generated in Step 1. The image is applied to the shape you selected with the Pen tool.

If a picture in your InDesign layout already has a clipping path, you may utilize it by choosing Display Import Options when you add the image to your layout.

If the image has more than one path, you can choose

which one to use by going to ObjectClipping PathOptions and then choosing either Alpha Channel or Clipping Path from the Type menu, depending on how the image is used.

If you add an image to your layout that was taken with a solid background, like a product shot for a catalog,

You can ask InDesign to make a clipping path for an image on a white background.Here's how it's done:

1. Using the Selection tool, choose a picture from your website with a solid backdrop, such as a white background.

2. Select the ObjectClipping Path Options option.

3. In the Clipping Path dialog box, choose Detect Edges from the Type drop-down option. Increase the threshold slider until the image's background vanishes.

4. Press the OK button.

The route is designed in such a way that the picture is seen and the backdrop is eliminated. The picture may be put over any other object to show any elements hidden behind it.

To expose items behind a clipping path, the object with the clipping path must be at the top-most layer or the top-most object inside its layer. You can confirm this by right-clicking the item and selecting ObjectArrangeBring to Front, as well as by accessing the layers panel via WindowLayers.

Item placement on the page

We demonstrate how to organize things on a page. But there are a few different methods to organize text or objects. This section discusses various methods to organize objects, giving you more flexibility over the arrangement of pieces in your document.

Orienting items

You can align visually in InDesign CC without using any additional tools or panels. When you use the Selection tool to pick and move things across a page when Smart Guides are enabled (they are by default), guidelines display automatically. These instructions appear when the selected item is aligned with other objects on the page or with the page itself. If seeing these annoying guides becomes a nuisance, go to EditPreferencesGuides & Pasteboard (Windows) or InDesignPreferencesGuides & Pasteboard (Mac) and uncheck the four settings under the Smart Guide Options title.

You may also use the Align panel to align things on a page: Choose WindowObject and LayoutAlign. This panel allows you to alter how items align to one another and to the general page. The Align panel has several buttons for controlling selected items. As you hover your mouse over a button, a tooltip will appear that describes how that button aligns components.

Look at the icon on the button if you're still unsure what each button performs after reading the corresponding tooltip. The icon might be useful in illustrating what the Align button does to selected items.

Here's how to align page elements:

1. Using the selection tool, choose numerous items on the page.
   To pick several items, hold down the Shift key while selecting each one.

When you click on an item on the page, it is selected. If your website lacks a few things, you can easily add a few new ones using the drawing tools.

2. Choose WindowObject and LayoutAlign. The Align panel is shown.

3. Choose the kind of alignment to apply to the chosen items.

   Click the Align Vertical Centers button to see what happens. Each item chosen aligns with the page's vertical center point.

Object distribution

We teach you how to align a few elements on a page in the previous step list, which is simple enough. But what if the things you're aligning aren't uniformly distributed? While their centers seem to be aligned, there is a significant gap between two of the photos and a tiny gap between the others. In such a situation, you must distribute and align the items. Distribute things on the page in various ways to space them relative to the page or to one another. Here's how it's done:

1. Use the Selection tool while holding the Shift key to choose items on a page that are not aligned or uniformly dispersed. When you click on an item, it is chosen. All of the things you choose will be aligned on the page.

2. Choose WindowObject and LayoutAlign if the Align panel isn't open. The Align panel is shown.

3. Choose the Distribute Horizontal Centers option, then select the

In the Align panel, click the Align Vertical Centers button just above it. The chosen objects are evenly distributed and horizontally aligned on the page.

Don't overlook the useful "Multiple Place" feature, which allows you to distribute and align objects on the fly! To place multiple images at once, use this handy option:

1. Click on FilePlace.

2. Hold down the Ctrl (Windows) or (Mac) key while selecting multiple images, and then

click the Open button.

3. Hold down Ctrl+Shift (Windows) or +Shift (Mac) before clicking to place the images.

The cursor appears in the form of a grid.

4. Create the rectangle in which you want your images by clicking and dragging.

Aligned with and disseminated throughout. The photos are automatically aligned and dispersed.

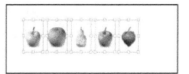

Exporting to PDF, Flash, and Printing

In addition to printing, InDesign publications may be exported into a variety of file formats. In this chapter, we'll look at how to prepare a file for delivery to a print provider as well as many of the many types of files you may make electronically from an InDesign page. Before printing a document, it's a good idea to double-check that you have everything you need, so let's start with the preflight option.

Preflight: Document Preparation for Printing

InDesign's Preflight tool confirms that everything you need to print your document is ready and accessible. It also displays details about the document you're printing, such as the typefaces, print settings, and inks utilized. Before printing your InDesign document, use Preflight to check for unlinked pictures and missing fonts.

Here's how to activate the Preflight feature:

1. Choose WindowOutputPreflight.
   The preflight window appears. Based on a study of the content, the Summary screen displays all current pictures and typefaces in the document.
2. Check that the On check box is checked and that the profile is set to [Basic] (working). These options do a basic preflight of the document, checking that all

pictures and typefaces are ready for printing and that there is nothing odd about the color that might cause frequent printing issues.

3. If any mistakes are found in the document, examine the error by clicking the page number provided to the right of the error in the preflight window. Typical issues, such as missing typefaces and overset text (text that does not fit entirely into a text frame), are all mentioned in the Preflight window and can usually be remedied quickly. It is much preferable to correct errors before printing them!

When you enable Preflight, a little green or red circle appears in the bottom-left corner of the document window. Green indicates that the document has been preflighted and no errors have been detected; however, red suggests that an error may have occurred. Just click the circle in the bottom-left corner of the Document window to enter the Preflight panel and look for any potential issues.

Your papers should be packaged

If you need to send your papers to a printer or another designer, make sure they have everything they need to continue working on the InDesign file. Here is when the Package command comes in handy.

Package collects all pictures and fonts used in the document, as well as a copy of the InDesign document, into a single package that you can quickly distribute to a print service provider or a colleague. You may also utilize this option to archive finished tasks to ensure that all required pieces are kept intact. Here's how it's done:

1. Choose a file package.
   The Package dialog box is shown. Based on a study of the content, the Summary screen displays all current pictures and typefaces in the document.
2. From the list on the left side of the dialog box, choose Fonts.

This screen displays a list of all typefaces in your document. Choose fonts from this list and then click the Locate Font button to find out where they are. After you complete the package, these typefaces are stored immediately in the package folder.

3. From the list on the left side of the dialog box, choose Links and Images.

The Links and Images screen displays a list of the pictures in your document.

Before packing the file, locate the picture, update it, and fix any broken links. If any photos are not correctly connected, your document is incomplete and will print with missing images.

4. Finally, at the bottom of the dialog box, click the "Package" button.

Your paper, along with all accompanying files, is stored in a folder. You may name the folder, indicate its location on your hard drive, and provide printing instructions.

If you're sending a file to a professional print service provider, you can either give them the original InDesign document or produce a high-quality PDF version that can be printed. It's a good idea to ask your print service provider what file types they like. By giving them an InDesign file, you allow them to fine-tune the document before printing, but if you submit a PDF, the document has restricted editing options. Various print providers need different file formats.

Understanding File Extensions

The kind of file you generate by exporting is determined by your demands.

The first step is to decide where you will utilize the exported file. For instance, you could need to

- ❖ Upload a picture of your InDesign document or page to the internet.
- ❖ Deliver the complete manuscript to someone who does not have InDesign but wishes to get it through email.

❖ Import the material into another application, such as Adobe Flash or Illustrator.

❖ Grab a certain kind of file and print it someplace else.

Exporting InDesign documents makes them "portable," allowing them to be utilized in multiple places, such as the web or another software.

You can choose from the numerous file formats supported by InDesign, and you can adjust many file-related parameters.

File Format	Description
JPEG (Joint Photographic Experts Group), PNG (Portable Network Graphics)	Either of these commonly used formats for compressed images is a good choice for creating a picture of an InDesign page to post on a website. This is only a picture and is good for something like a thumbnail image representing a document. Don't use this if you want someone to actually read the InDesign file on the web — for that you'll want to export to HTML or PDF. This is simply a picture preview of what a document page looks like. *(continued)*

File Format	Description
EPS (Encapsulated PostScript)	A self-contained image file that contains high-resolution printing information about all the text and graphics used on a page. This format is commonly used for high-quality printing when you need to have an image of an InDesign page used within another document — such as a picture of a book cover created with InDesign that needs to appear in a promotional catalog — so that you can use an EPS of the book cover in your layout.
XML (Extensible Markup Language)	Lets you separate the content from the layout so that all the content on a page can be repurposed and used in different ways — online or in print. Corporations commonly use XML for storing their product data when they have a large amount of information — such as thousands of items in a catalog.
FLA and SWF	Use the FLA (Flash) file format if you want to take your InDesign document into Flash, add interactivity to it, and continue to edit the document. Use the SWF (ShockWave Flash) format to deliver the PDF for viewing in a web browser as an SWF file for viewing (but not editing). Note that many web browsers no longer support the SWF file format, so use this option only if you are certain the recipient is able to view the file.
PDF (Portable Document Format)	Used to exchange documents with users on different computer systems and operating systems. This format is used extensively for distributing files such as e-books and brochures. You may need to distribute the file to a wide audience or to a service provider for printing. Anyone who has installed Adobe Reader (also known as Acrobat Reader) on a computer can view your document. You can export PDFs designed for printing by selecting PDF (Print). Select PDF (Interactive) if your PDF contains hyperlinks or movies and will be distributed online instead of being printed.
Rich or Plain text (text files)	Can include formatting (Rich) or plain text only (Plain). A text file is a simple way to export content. If you need the text from your document only to incorporate or send elsewhere, you can export it as plain (Text Only), tagged, or rich text. If you need to send a document to someone who doesn't have InDesign, exporting it as text may be a good option.
EPUB	Use the e-pub file format to create electronic books that can be read using an electronic book reader, including devices such as the nook or iPad, or using any e-book reader software. With additional conversion, this file can also be read on the Amazon Kindle.

File Format	Description
HTML	Use the HTML file format to export a document as HTML (HyperText Markup Language), which is the language used by web browsers. Documents exported using this option typically require some HTML editing for formatting and design, which you can do using Adobe Dreamweaver.
IDML	Use the InDesign Markup Language option to export InDesign documents in a format that can be read by earlier versions of InDesign. For example, if you have a colleague using InDesign CS6 and you want to provide him with your document, but you are using InDesign CC, export the document using the IDML option, and he will be able to open it. If you simply save the file, the older version of InDesign is not able to open the document.

InDesign can export JPG, PDF, and EPS files, which may subsequently be loaded into other software applications. After importing the photographs into a separate graphics application, you may export them for usage in print or utilize them on the web. It all depends on how you export the document and the settings you choose.

After deciding on a file format, consider how to export these files and the various types of parameters you can manage. The remainder of this chapter demonstrates how to export various file types from InDesign.

Publications Export

The Export dialog box allows you to export publications. After opening it by selecting FileExport, you may choose the file format, name, and destination. After entering a name, a location, and an export format, click Save. A new dialog box appears, where you may make file format-specific adjustments. In the sections that follow, we'll go through some of the most prevalent file types for export.

Creating PDF files for printing

If you want to ensure that what you developed is precisely what readers see—even if they don't have InDesign—create a PDF copy of your project. A PDF file's editing capabilities are likewise limited, making it unlikely that your document will be updated. If you select to export a PDF document, you have several choices for customizing the document. With InDesign, you may customize the amount of compression in the document, the markings and bleeds, and the security settings. To export to PDF, follow these steps:

1. Select FileExport. The Export dialog box is shown.
2. Choose a place for saving the file and then input a new filename.

   If you're using Windows, use the Save In drop-down list to go to a spot on your hard drive and name the file in the File Name text box.

   On a Mac, type a name for the file in the Save As text box and choose a location from the Where drop-down list.
3. At the bottom of the Export window, choose Adobe PDF (Print) from the Save As type (Windows) or Format (Mac) drop-down list.
4. Click the Save button.

   The General Settings screen is

available in the Export Adobe PDF dialog box.

5. Choose an Adobe PDF preset from the drop-down list. These settings are simple to apply. They're the same if you're acquainted with Adobe Acrobat and the Adobe Distiller features.

The presets in the Adobe PDF Presets drop-down list modify the specific export parameters of a document automatically. Choose Smallest File Size from the options, for example, if you want to show your work online, or High Quality Print if you intend to print the PDF on home printers. If you want to have the PDF professionally printed, choose Press Quality.

6. Choose "None" from the Standard drop-down list.

Keep it at "None" unless you're familiar with the PDF/X rules for distributing ads.

7. In the Range text box, enter the start page (and then a hyphen) and the end page to export a range of pages. Nonconsecutive pages may also be exported by separating the page numbers with a comma. All pages are exported by default.

8. From the Compatibility drop-down list, choose a compatibility option for the PDF. The compatibility options define what kind of reader is needed to see the document. Setting compatibility to Acrobat 5 guarantees that your PDF files may be viewed by a broad range of people. If you choose compatibility for a higher version, certain older PDF viewers may be unable to comprehend some features in your document. Setting

this value to Acrobat 5 or later assures that the PDF file may be viewed by anybody who has installed Adobe Reader or Acrobat within the last 10 years.

9. Choose whether to include thumbnails and whether to optimize the document, then decide which types of items to include in the file by checking the box to the left of the choices in the Include section. Additional options control the incorporation of bookmarks, links, and other file features. You don't need to bother with picking these choices until you've added any of these components. You may wish to incorporate thumbnail previews; however, Acrobat automatically builds thumbnails when the file is viewed, so this might increase the file size needlessly. To view the security screen, click Security in the list on the left

of the Export Adobe PDF dialog box. Here, you may set passwords to open the document. You may also provide a password that must be entered in order to print or change the PDF file.

10. To export the file, click the Export option.

The file is saved to the specified location.

EPS file exporting

You may export EPS files from InDesign, which are handy for loading into other products. Since EPS files are single-page graphics files, each exported InDesign page is stored as a distinct EPS file.

There is no need to export an EPS file in order to insert an InDesign file into another InDesign file! If you're making classified pages or any other page that includes other InDesign pages, you may avoid a few steps by selecting FilePlace and then the InDesign file.

While InDesign can import InDesign files or even PDFs into a layout, the only reason to export to EPS is to make an image for an older program or database that doesn't support newer file types.

Here is how you export EPS files:

1. Select FileExport.
   The Export dialog box is shown.
2. Go to the directory on your hard drive where you want to store the EPS files, type a new filename, and pick EPS from the Save As type (Windows) or format (Mac) drop-down list; click Save.
   The dialog box labeled "Export EPS" appears.
3. Choose a single page or a range of pages to export.
   Choose All Pages to export all pages, or Ranges to export a specific range of pages. Choose the "Spreads" radio option to export spreads as a single file.
   Whenever you create several EPS files (for example, exporting more than one page of an InDesign

document), the file is saved with the filename, an underscore, and the page number.

4. Choose a color mode from the Color drop-down list; from the Embed Fonts drop-down list, choose how to embed fonts.

Choose "Leave Unchanged" from the Color drop-down box to keep the InDesign document's color mode. Color modes include CMYK (Cyan, Magenta, Yellow, Black), Gray (Grayscale), and RGB (Red, Green, Blue).

Choose Subset from the Embed Fonts drop-down box to embed just the characters used in the file. When you print the file, all fonts in the file are loaded if you pick Complete. When you choose None, a reference to the font's location is put into the file.

5. Choose whether or not to produce a preview for the file by using the Preview drop-down list.

If an EPS file cannot be shown, a preview (a tiny thumbnail picture) is helpful. For example, if you're browsing an image library, you'll see a tiny thumbnail image of the EPS file; this way, whether you utilize the image or open it on your computer, you'll know what the file looks like.

Choose TIFF from the Preview drop-down list to produce a preview; select None to not generate a preview.

6. To export the files, click the Export option.

The files are saved to the directory you specified in Step 2.

JPEG and PNG file export

InDesign documents may be exported as JPG or PNG files. These file types are frequently used in web publishing and may be used to upload an image of an InDesign document or page to the internet. You may export a single item on the specified page as a JPEG or PNG picture, or you can export full pages and spreads. JPEG and PNG files enable you to compress full-color or black-and-white photos efficiently, which is important if you require a picture of an InDesign page to display on the web.

Follow these procedures to export a JPEG or PNG image:

1. If you wish to export a page or spread, pick an item on the page or ensure that no object is selected.

2. Select FileExport. The Export dialog box is shown.

3. Enter a filename, go to the location on your hard drive where you wish to save the file, and pick JPEG or PNG from the Save As type (Windows) or format (Mac) drop-down list; click Save.
The "Export JPG or PNG" dialog box appears.

4. To export a page, click the Pages radio button and put the page number in the Range text box; to export the selected item, make sure the Selection option is selected.
The Selection option is only available if a

selection was made in Step 1.

5. Choose an image quality and format method from the Image Quality and Format Method drop-down menus to export.

When you export a JPEG or PNG image, the Image Quality drop-down list determines how much compression is applied. Select from the following options:

- Maximum: Produces the greatest file size and best quality picture.

- High: Produces a higher-quality picture with a bigger file size.

- Medium: Produces a picture with a medium file size and quality.

- Low: Produces a smaller file with worse quality since it contains less picture information.

When you choose the baseline format from the Format Method drop-down menu, the full picture is downloaded before it can be shown in a web browser. Select Progressive to view the image in a web browser in a progressive full presentation as it downloads.

When you create a PNG image, the Format Method choices do not display.

6. Choose the export option.

Step 3: The file is exported and stored at the location you chose.

Flash exporting

You can export an InDesign document as a Flash Professional file (FLA) that can be modified in Flash CC or as a Flash Player (SWF) file that can be read in Flash Player (but not edited).

Several recent web browsers do not support Flash, including the browsers on the Apple iPhone and iPad, and certain Microsoft browsers have restricted support. Since the Flash file format is in decline, you should think carefully about whether you want to export to Flash at all. But, since Flash export is still a possibility, we'll go through it here. Follow these instructions to export to the Flash Player (SWF) format:

1. Select FileExport. The Export dialog box is shown.
2. Choose a place for the files to be saved, type a new filename, and select Flash Player (SWF) from the Save As type (Windows) or Format (Mac) drop-down list. Export the file in the Flash Professional (FLA) format if you need to incorporate video, music, animation, or complicated

interaction, since you can then use Flash Professional to tweak and edit the file until it suits your specific demands.

Although the SWF format creates an SWF version of your document that can be read online rapidly, it does not allow you to revise and amend your selections after exporting.

With the Export SWF dialog box, you may define the output size, which pages to include, and which conversion and compression options to use.

3. Determine the size of the exported file.

If you don't want to adjust the size of the exported file, choose Scale and leave the drop-down list at 100%. Instead, select Fit To from the drop-down menu, or select Width and enter your own proportions in the Width and Height drop-down menus.

4. Choose the page or pages to export. Choose All Pages to export the whole document; choose Range and provide a page number to export just a single page or pages.

5. Choose the interactivity choices you want by specifying whether you want all interactive options or simply those that influence appearance.

6. Choose whether to export Page Transitions or a list of included transitions such as Dissolve or Wipe.

7. Choose if an interactive page

curl should show in the upper right corner of the document page.

8. Click OK to save your InDesign work as an SWF file.

Text file exporting

Text may be extracted from an InDesign document and altered or used elsewhere. Depending on the content in your document, the text formats differ somewhat.

Follow these procedures to export text:

1. From the toolbox, pick the Text tool and select some text inside a text frame in your project, or set the cursor within a text frame where you wish to export all the content. To export text, the cursor must be in a text frame.

2. Choose FileExport. The Export dialog box is shown.

3. Specify a filename, choose a location for the file, and choose Text Only from the Save As type (Windows) or format (Mac) drop-down box; then click Save.

The Text Export Options dialog box is shown.

4. Choose an export platform and encoding.

   To configure the PC or Mac operating system compatibility, choose either PC or Macintosh from the Platform drop-down box. From the Encoding drop-down box, choose an encoding technique for the platform you want to use; you may use Default Platform or Unicode.

Unicode, the worldwide character encoding standard, is compatible with all major operating systems. Encoding, or how characters are represented in digital format, is simply a set of rules that dictate how the character set is represented by linking each character with a certain code sequence.

5. Click the Export button.

   Step 3: The file is exported and stored at the location you chose.

Making a Print of Your Art

You can print your work from an InDesign document in a variety of ways, using a variety of printers and methods. You have two options: utilize your home or business printer or send your work to a professional printing service.

The quality of output available from printers and printing services varies.

The sections that follow examine the various methods for preparing a document for printing as well as the types of problems that may arise during this process.

The Meaning of "Bleed"

If you want an image or color span to stretch all the way to the edge of a page, you bleed it off the edge of the document. Bleeding is the process of extending the print area slightly beyond the page's border into the region that will be cut and removed during the printing process. (Professional printers may print your papers on larger-than-necessary page sizes and then clip off the excess paper.) You may also bleed your own work. Turn on crop and bleed markings when creating to highlight where the page has to be cut to ensure that the picture bleeds far enough off the border of the page area. This is covered in the next section.

Printing and proofreading at home or at the workplace

Since many InDesign works are intended to be professionally printed, the print options provided are fairly strong. They are not complex just because they are strong. We've simplified the options for you here:

To enter the Print dialog box, choose FilePrint.

From the Printer drop-down option, choose the printer you want to use. If you don't have a printer, choose Adobe PDF from the Printer drop-down selection to proceed with the procedures below.

There are several printing choices accessible in the list on the left side of the Print dialog box. As you click an item, the dialog box changes to show the options for the chosen item. To learn more about these typical printing choices, click on the links below:

❖ Generally speaking, specify the number of copies to print and the number of pages to print for the document. To print from the last page to the first page, use the Reverse Order check box. Choose an option from the Sequence drop-down menu to print just even or odd pages rather than all pages. Choose the Spreads radio option if you're dealing with spreads that need to be printed on a single page.

❖ Setup: Choose the size of the paper, the orientation (portrait or landscape), and the scale. You may scale a page to be 1,000% of its original size or as small as 1% of its original size. You may (optionally) limit the width and height scales so that the page maintains the same ratio.

When utilizing paper that is larger than the document you've prepared, the Page Position drop-down list comes in handy. This option allows you to center the page on larger sheets of paper.

❖ Marks and Bleed: Toggle on or off several of the document's printing markings, such as crop, bleed, and registration marks. For example, if a bleed runs over the page's limits and you need to demonstrate where to crop each page, you may wish to display these markings. You can get a preview of how the page will appear when printed, and you can choose whether to display page information (such as the filename and date) on each page.

❖ Output: Choose whether to print pages as a separation or a composite, with which inks (if using separations), and with or without trapping. Using the parameters you provide, InDesign may divide and print documents as plates (which are used in commercial printing).

❖ Graphics: Regulate how the document's visuals and fonts are printed.

The Send Data drop-down list manages bitmap images and determines how much data is transmitted to the printer from these pictures. Here are some other printing options:

- All: This option sends all bitmap data. Use this for the finest quality printing, but be aware that high-resolution photographs may take a long time to print.

- Subsampling Optimization: Sends as much picture data as the printer can handle. If you're experiencing trouble printing high-quality photographs while selecting the All option, try this.

- Proxy: Prints lower-quality photos primarily for preview purposes.

- None: Prints an X through placeholder boxes. This option allows you to rapidly print a layout proof to get a quick idea of a page's design.

❖ Color Management: Choose how you want color to be

handled when it is produced. If you have output device profiles installed on your system, you can select them here. Commercial print suppliers and vendors with important color demands are more likely to employ color management. It's a complicated issue—whole volumes have been written on color management—and we don't have the room to go into it here.

❖ Advanced: Choose how photos should be supplied to the printer.

If you're not acquainted with the Open Prepress Interface (OPI), you may leave this option alone. The OPI technique, also known as image-swapping technology, enables low-resolution photos imported into InDesign to be exchanged with the high-resolution version for output. It's a very specialized option utilized by commercial print suppliers that operate with a huge number of photographs, such as catalog print sellers.

Whether you utilize a drop shadow, feather an object in InDesign, or apply transparency to any objects, flattening must be handled, even if they were generated in Photoshop or Illustrator.

For desktop printers, use the Medium Resolution option, and for professional press output, use the High Resolution preset.

❖ Summary: You can't change anything, but you can get an excellent summary of all your print settings.

If you wish to save the changes you've made after finishing your settings, click the Save Preset option. If you anticipate printing more papers with similar settings on a regular basis, utilizing the Save Preset option may be a huge time saver.

When you click the Save Preset button, the Save Preset dialog box appears, allowing you to give the settings a new name. The stored preset may be selected from the Print Preset drop-down list in the Print dialog box the next time you print a document.

When you're ready to print the document, click the "Print" button at the bottom of the Print dialog box.

Creating Digital Documents Using HTML and EPUB

InDesign was designed over a decade ago as a tool for generating printed documents, not digital documents and electronic books.

Adobe included the ability to produce digital documents for distribution on tablets, e-readers, and the web with InDesign CS6. The vast bulk of the new capabilities included in the previous version of InDesign were aimed at generating digital documents.

Since tablet publishing is still in its early stages, processes, tools, and features are still in their infancy. We find the process a little clunky in certain circumstances — and the features introduced to InDesign seem like an afterthought — but unless you want to learn to write HTML5 and CSS3, the Creative Cloud tools are your best choice for getting your material sent onto a tablet or e-reading device.

Digital documents may be formatted and optimized to show on a range of devices. We will look at two of them:

- ❖ HTML: HTML is replacing PDF and SWF (Flash) as the traditional means to disseminate electronic copies of documents published on the web, as web pages, for two key reasons:
  - HTML, unlike PDF and Flash, may be viewed on any device that has a web browser.
  - The forthcoming HTML5 and CSS3 standards enable content to be changed according on the device or browser used to view the page. A separate layout, for example, may exist for vertical and horizontal display.
- ❖ EPUB: While HTML is becoming the preferred method for distributing documents in web browsers, EPUB is the standard for electronic books

that can be accessed online and offline, and we will look at producing documents for distribution using the EPUB format in this chapter.

Content Transformation for Digital Distribution

It takes more than simply picking an output type and hitting the Export button to create a digital document. To create successful papers, you must design them with the requirements of the device on which they will be viewed in mind.

To do this, you may either use different layouts to customize the document's layout for certain devices, such as an iPad vertical or iPad horizontal layout.

Instead, you may use Liquid Layout to define a set of rules that adjust the layout to function on different devices.

Generating Electronic Documents

Nowadays, you should design your papers with digital dissemination in mind. If you need to convert a print document to an electronic format, make a copy of the original InDesign document and work on the copy as a separate electronic document. You may distribute books to e-reading devices like the nook, Kindle, and iPad by creating an e-pub.

Follow these procedures to convert an existing print document to a digital document layout:

1. Open the current document and choose FileSave As, then name the duplicate.
   Choose a name that is relevant to your intended distribution. Try using phrases like EPUB or iPad in the filename to differentiate the electronic edition from the print version.

If you're producing an e-pub document for a book that's just text and will be read on a variety of devices, you may skip Step 1 since you don't need to include layout information or device specifications for particular devices. Continue using the following steps for e-pub publications that demand carefully structured layouts.

2. Choose FileDocument Setup. Choose Digital Publication from the Intent drop-down menu in the Document Setup box, and then pick the required Page Size and orientation (vertical or horizontal).

3. Close the Document Setup box by clicking OK, and then choose FileSave to save your changes.

4. Browse through the content and make layout changes depending on the available page size. To move things, use the Selection tool, and to create pages, use the Pages panel.

5. Choose WindowArticles to display the Articles panel. Drag items from your layout into the Articles panel using the Selection tool to define the order in which they will be presented in an e-pub. If you don't want anything in the digital edition of the book, just don't drag it into the Articles panel. After dragging all objects to be

exported to the Articles panel, save your project.

Developing different layouts

With the Pages panel, you may design different horizontal and vertical layouts for your page. When you convert your page to HTML, it includes Cascading Style Sheets (CSS) information that modifies the layout depending on how it is viewed.

Follow these steps to create a different layout:

1. In the Pages panel, click to choose an existing page that you wish to change the layout of.

For example, if you have a horizontal layout and wish to make a vertical version, pick the horizontal layout.

2. Choose Build Alternative Layout from the Pages panel menu. Name the alternative layout, then enter the page properties and click OK.

The alternative layout is used to produce a new page, and the content from the original page is replicated and linked to the duplicate page.

3. Adjust the page element arrangement on the alternative layout as required.

Any text and picture frames that were replicated onto the alternative layout have a link sign in the upper-left corner.

This shows that the alternative layout's content and graphics are related to the original. Modifications made to the original layout's items are mirrored on the alternative layout.

A yellow triangle shows instead of the link sign if an item in the alternative layout differs from the original layout. When you double-click the yellow triangle, the item in the alternative layout gets synced with the original layout.

Designing liquid layouts

The Liquid Layout feature, which was inspired by the concept of Responsive Design in the web design community, allows you to utilize InDesign as a tool for building web-adaptable layouts. The Liquid Layout feature assists in the creation of HTML pages and CSS that are responsive to different web browsers and mobile devices.

To utilize Liquid Layout, go through the following steps:

1. Choose the Page Tool and click to pick any page with content.
   This instructs InDesign on how to alter each page when it is exported to HTML.
2. Go to the Liquid Page Rule area in the Control panel. Choose the Scale option to keep all information on your website even if the page size is reduced.
3. Put the Liquid Layout to the test by continuing to use the Page tool to click and drag the page handles and see how the items on the page change. If you used the Scale option, the page objects should all shrink in size when you shrink the page using the Page tool, emulating how the website would appear on a mobile web browser.

Additional characteristics of digital documents

Employ the following features to make your digital documents more interactive:

❖ The Animation panel may be used to add motion to elements on your page. You may, for example, have an item fade in while the page loads, or fade out and vanish. Choose WindowInteractive Animation to open this panel, and then add animation to individual objects by selecting them and selecting an animation option from the Preset drop-down menu in the Animation panel.

❖ Timing Panel: Use the Timing panel to make changes to animations produced in the Animation panel. Choose WindowInteractive Timing to open this panel. Use the Event drop-down list to indicate when an object's animation happens, and the Delay option to describe whether or not the animation should wait before occurring.

- ❖ Buttons and Forms: Use this panel to turn text or pictures into interactive buttons that appear when the InDesign page is saved to PDF. Choose WindowInteractive Buttons and Forms to open this panel. Buttons may be coupled with actions, causing something to happen when they are clicked. A button, for example, may play a video or music, go to a certain website, or print a form when pressed. This panel may also be used to transform text frames to text fields, allowing you to build PDF forms in InDesign.

HTML exporting

When you export an InDesign project to HTML, you can share it on the web so that it may be seen on a range of devices. The HTML file generated by InDesign is likewise readily editable. Just open the file in Dreamweaver

Follow these procedures to convert an InDesign document to HTML:

1. Choose FileExport while an InDesign document is open. The Export dialog box is shown.

2. Choose HTML from the Save as Type (Windows) or Format (Mac) drop-down box. Finally, choose a spot on your hard drive or network to store the document. In the File Name section of the Export dialog box, type a name for the HTML file.

3. Choose the Save option.

   The HTML Export Options dialog box displays, displaying the General choices for editing. You may choose whether to export merely the selection (if you have anything chosen) or the complete document in this dialog box. You may also lay out how to deal with bullets and numbers.

4. On the left column, click Picture to view choices for storing optimal photos. Keep the Image Conversion drop-down list set to

Automatic to allow InDesign determine whether a picture should be saved as a GIF or JPEG file, or select the format for all images. This conversion is required because the file formats used by InDesign may not be compatible with certain web browsers.

5. On the left column, choose Advanced to specify how Cascading Style Sheets (CSS) are handled – whether you want them to be used or to reference (link to) an external CSS style.

6. If you want the file to open in your normal web browser, go back to the General option on the left and choose See HTML after Exporting. Next choose the Export option.The file has been exported.

The file opens in your browser if you choose See HTML after Exporting. Alternatively, you may now instantly access and modify the HTML file in Dreamweaver.

EPUB Exporting

The EPUB file format is used by books shown on iBooks, Nook devices, Kobo readers, and Sony eReaders. Books shown on the Kindle begin as e-pub files but are then converted into Amazon's proprietary Kindle format. The bottom line is that if you want to make electronic books, you must first learn how to generate EPUB files. Here's how to make an e-book with InDesign:

1. While an InDesign document is open, select FileExport.

The Export dialog box is shown.

2. Choose EPUB from the Save as type (Windows) or format (Mac) drop-down list, and then browse to a spot on your hard drive or network to store the document. In the File Name section of the Export dialog box, enter a name for the EPUB file.

3. Choose the "Save" option.

The EPUB Export Options dialog box appears, displaying the General editing options. Here's a rundown of the most important options under the General page when establishing an e-pub:

- Version: If you're exporting an e-pub with multimedia, choose EPUB 3.0. Alternatively, EPUB 2.0.1 may be used. While Adobe provides a proprietary EPUB 3.0 format with layout options, it is incompatibl e with the majority of common reading devices and should be avoided unless you have a special requirement to export in this format.
- Cover: If you want InDesign to build the e-pub cover image, specify whether it should utilize the first page of

the manuscript or a particular image file if the cover artwork is stored elsewhere on your hard drive or network.

- Navigation: Choose TOC Style if you want InDesign to automaticall y build a table of contents that users may utilize to explore

the e-pub file more simply.

- Margins: Enter any padding between the text and the outer edge of the reading device.

- See EPUB after exporting: opens and displays the e-pub in the default EPUB reader when InDesign creates the e-pub file.

4. In the EPUB Export Settings dialog box, choose the Image tab.

Under the Image tab, set the resolution at which pictures should be made for the e-book. Additionally, describe where photos should be displayed on the page, as well as any space that should be placed before or after images.

5. Go to the Advanced tab.

When making the e-pub, make the following changes under the Advanced tab as needed:

- Divide Document: Choose the paragraph style to specify where each part should be separated if you wish to break a big document into different chapters. Alternatively, leave it at the default setting of "Do Not Split."

- EPUB Metadata: EPUB readers employ document metadata to describe the book title, publisher, ISBN, and other information. In the Unique ID section, put the publisher's name and the ISBN number for your book.
- CSS Options:

You may include a style sheet if you have prepared Cascading Style Sheets (CSS) to manage the formatting of your EPUB files. Instead, by checking the Include Style Definitions box, you may have InDesign add style definitions and produce a CSS file. Deselect

Include Embeddable Fonts under this same option since many electronic reading devices disregard them and some electronic book shops reject files with embedded fonts.

Document metadata may be added in the Document Information field. To get to this, select FileDocument Information.

6. Press the OK button.

The e-book is finished. If you checked the "View EPUB after Exporting" option, the EPUB file will be opened in your default EPUB reader.

Since e-books employ HTML as their base, the EPUB Export Options dialog box resembles the HTML Export window.

Electronic book readers are simply

specialized browsers built to show HTML and CSS-formatted books. The compressed folder with the EPUB file extension contains all of the HTML and CSS content for an EPUB file.

www.ingramcontent.com/pod-product-compliance
Lightning Source LLC
LaVergne TN
LVHW051221050326
832903LV00028B/2192